THE BEST WAY TO DEAL WITH WINES

Let The Best Way to Deal with Wines transform your wine experience and inspire a lifelong appreciation for the artistry of winemaking.

LISA HOSEIN

All rights reserved. No Part of this publication may be reproduced, distributed, or circulated in any form or by any means, including photocopying, recording, or other electronic methods, without prior written permission of the publisher, except in the case of short quotations embodied in critical reviews and certain other non-commercial uses permitted by copyright law.

INTRODUCTION

At its most fundamental level, wine constitutes a blend of countless distinct molecules in a perpetual state of variation, a characteristic that imparts the quality of being a living, breathing entity. The identity and concentration of these diverse compounds at any specific moment rely on every conceivable factor, from the vine and the soil to the climatic conditions of that season, the entire production process, how a bottle has been stored, and the duration a poured glass or opened bottle has had to aerate prior to being savored. Our perception of its flavor is equally malleable, influenced by its temperature, our emotional state, our recent gastronomic experiences, and our receptors' ability to differentiate those myriad molecules at all. Consequently, if we are to contemplate how to unravel the intricacies of wine, we must commence by comprehending this beverage from the perspective of its chemistry, as it is molecules and their capabilities that lie at the core of the issue.

This text by Waterhouse, Sacks, and Jeffery serves as an exceptional foundation for such explorations. Chemistry alone can appear overwhelmingly intricate, yet what these prominent scholars have effortlessly achieved over the course of 33 chapters is a method not just to appreciate, but also to comprehend the pertinent chemistry and chemical phenomena that influence every aspect of wine from an analytical, organic, and physical viewpoint. This achievement stems from an approach that initially outlines all the distinct compound classes present in wine, their reactivities, and their contributions to the final flavor profile. The text subsequently advances to the production process and elucidates, at a suitably detailed chemical level, not only the fermentation and overall production process but also how each step and specific choices along the way can affect which molecules, and in what quantities, manifest in the final product. Finally, by presenting the most recent scholarship, the authors illuminate the frontiers of wine chemistry research, signposting opportunities for readers to pursue further avenues of exploration if they are inclined.

Whether a novice, a connoisseur, a production enthusiast, or an aspiring professional, this meticulously crafted text provides all readers with the opportunity to deepen their knowledge of and appreciation for this remarkable beverage, along with the potential to contribute to enhancements in its future enjoyment. It is certainly hoped that these authors will continue to supplement and refine this already outstanding work in the years ahead through additional editions as the understanding of wine chemistry continues to expand. Nonetheless, for now, commendations are warranted for their efforts in successfully distilling diverse knowledge gleaned from numerous branches of chemistry into a completely accessible, engaging, and pedagogically robust approach to the science of wine.

FORWARD

Possessing backgrounds in conventional branches of chemistry (organic, analytical, physical), we now consider it a privilege to compose a discourse on wine chemistry. Not only is wine chemistry a topic that captivates and provokes thought, it also serves as a remarkable medium for dialogue – we frequently engage with colleagues, visitors, and acquaintances who express their affection for wine and its intricacies. Such intricacy can be fascinating, yet it may also act as an impediment to deeper comprehension, whether wine represents a pastime or a profession.

Wine chemistry is imparted in an increasing number of institutions as a component of enology and viticulture programs, in addition to traditional undergraduate chemistry departments as an elective offering. Moreover, numerous individuals within wine production and related sectors (e. g., suppliers) anticipate making science-based decisions or recommendations. Keeping this in consideration, we recognized the necessity for a publication that could illustrate to a reader how to apply a fundamental understanding of chemistry to rationally elucidate – and, more importantly, forecast – the variety evident among wines.

Rather than solely presenting a description of wine constituents, or concentrating on sensory attributes, analytical facets, or processing challenges, we address the categories of chemical and biochemical reactions that frequently take place in wine – in essence, we analyze winemaking results through the framework of chemical principles. In pursuing this aim, we seek to aid students, winemakers, and others in anticipating the impacts of wine treatments and procedures, or interpreting experimental outcomes, grounded in an understanding of the principal reactions that may occur in wine. We presume only a minimal prior acquaintance with wine and winemaking, but anticipate basic chemistry knowledge, including organic chemistry, while we acknowledge that our readers might have overlooked one (or several) lessons from these courses.

The chemical variety of wine

How many options does a purchaser possess when acquiring a wine? In the United States, all wines available must possess a Certificate of Label Approval (COLA) from the Alcohol and Tobacco Tax and Trade Bureau (TTB), and in 2013, the TTB sanctioned over 93,000 COLA applications. Due to the fact that numerous wines are vintage items, meaning a new label will be generated for each harvest year, the actual quantity of wines accessible in wine retailers across the United States may be nearer to 250,000. In contrast to commodity items where manufacturers aim for uniformity (e. g. , soybeans, milk), variation in specialty items like wine is not only accepted – it is valued and celebrated. Consumers anticipate that wines with distinct labels should possess different aromas, flavors, and appearances; from a chemist's standpoint, consumers expect wines to exhibit varying chemical compositions. The exploration of wine chemistry involves examining these disparities – elucidating how there can be hundreds of thousands, if not millions, of unique wine compositions, and enhancing a winemaker's comprehension of how the multitude of selections they encounter can result in these variations.

TREATS

MAKES 16 There was old-fashioned simplicity long before Pop-Tarts had fancy flavors and elaborate decorations. I remember dragging a chair halfway across the floor of my kitchen so I could get my favorite Pop-Tart high up in the cabinet, far back, behind the "healthy" breakfast items: cinnamon and brown sugar. Too eager to even consider trusting that the toaster oven will warm it up, I would eat the mixture edges in a coordinated example moving clockwise around the tart, then the top layer, lastly the base layer with the filling. Nirvana. I've remade my favorite breakfast treat with an adult pastry chef twist now that I'm older (and kids like them too!).

3 cups regular baking flour

2 tablespoons granulated sugar

2 teaspoons genuine salt

1 cup (2 sticks) unsalted margarine, cut into 3D squares and freezing

7 tablespoons ice water

1½ teaspoons white vinegar

An additional 1 enormous egg, at room temperature

¾ cup Pop Jam or great quality locally acquired jam

⅓ cup turbinado sugar

1 Utilizing an electric blender fitted with the oar append ment, blend the flour, sugar, and salt until mixed. Mix on medium-low speed for four minutes after adding the butter, or until very small butter pieces are visible. Join 6 tablespoons of the ice water and the vinegar and add it to the flour blend. Mix on medium speed until dough crumbles are formed that are moist.

2 Transfer the dough and any remaining flour to a work surface, and knead six to eight times until a smooth dough forms. The Pop Ts won't be easy to make if you overwork the dough.

3 Divide the dough in half; if you have a scale, weigh the two halves. After that, shape each half into flat, even rectangles and wrap one half in plastic wrap to prevent it from drying out.

4 Put an enormous piece of material paper on a work surface. A second sheet of parchment paper should be placed on top of the dough's unwrapped rectangle. Roll the dough into a rectangle that is 1/8 of an inch thick and slightly larger than 14 x 10 inches. At intervals, peel away the paper, lightly dust the dough with flour, and reposition the paper so that there are no wrinkles. Make an effort to maintain a neat rectangle; doing so will assist you in maintaining an accurate Pop T count.

5 Transfer the dough to a baking sheet lined with parchment paper and refrigerate for 30 to 45 minutes, or until the dough is very firm. If you

want the dough to chill more quickly, freeze it for about 15 minutes. Continue with the remaining dough.

6 Use nonstick liners or parchment paper to line two baking sheets. In a small bowl, whisk together the egg and the remaining 1 tablespoon of ice water until well combined.

7 Arrange each sheet of dough on a work surface one at a time and peel away the top parchment. Cut the dough sheets into 10 x 14-inch rectangles with a ruler and a small, sharp knife or pizza cutter. Cut every one into sixteen 2½ × 3½-inch square shapes.

8 Carefully remove 16 rectangles from the parchment with a metal spatula and space them about an inch apart on the baking sheets that have been prepared. Fill a baked good pack (no tip required) with the jam, pipe an insufficient tablespoon down the focal point of every square shape, and spread the jam to about ½ inch from the edge of every square shape. (You can likewise utilize a spoon to do this, however I believe it's quicker and more straightforward to utilize a cake sack.) Apply the beaten egg to the borders.

9 Cautiously place the excess square shapes over the jam and tenderly press out all the air. Trim any uneven edges with a small knife if you want perfect-looking pop tarts. Crimp the edges to seal with a fork's tines. Cover the tarts with saran wrap and slide the baking sheets once more into the fridge for 1 to 2 hours, or freeze again for 30 minutes to 60 minutes, until the mixture is

exceptionally firm. Refrigerate the remaining egg mixture under a cover.

10 Position racks in the upper center and lower center of the broiler, and preheat the stove to 350°F (325°F if utilizing a convection broiler).

11 Make three small slits in the top of each pop tart with a small knife, each about 12 inches across; Sprinkle with the turbinado sugar and brush with the remaining beaten egg. The bottoms should be golden brown after baking for 34 to 36 minutes (or 20 to 23 minutes if using a convection oven).

12 Exchange the baking sheets to wire racks and let cool. You'll be enticed to eat the tarts right out of the broiler yet DON'T! As of now the jam is atomic hot.

13 Reheat the tarts in a toaster after storing them for up to three days in an airtight container at room temperature.

MAKES 20 PIECES This is my unsurpassed most loved extravagance that makes everything all around great. the world's finest candy In a nutshell.

Flashback to when I was five years of age, living in Upper east Philadelphia, and it was Halloween. My mother made me a fastidious jokester outfit that I could scarcely move in. Steven, my brother, and I dumped our candy bags on the dining room table after trick-or-treating. Mother permitted us to keep just our #1 confections, and she would take all the other things to attempt to impart to her collaborators (however I'm unsure she truly shared!). It was hard to choose, but nothing else really mattered once I got to that bright orange box of Reese's Peanut Butter Cups.

My take on the classic has a flavorful peanut butter and a texture that is silky smooth. Extras, if you have any, make a stellar dessert beating.

8 ounces clashing chocolate (ideally Valrhona Caraïbe 66%)

6 tablespoons (¾ stick) unsalted margarine, at room temperature

⅓ cup (pressed) dim earthy colored sugar

1 cup confectioners' sugar

1 teaspoon genuine salt

1 cup rich peanut butter (ideally natural), at room temperature

1 Line the base and sides of a 8½ × 4½-inch portion container with material paper or foil, and oil it gently (ideally with Pam). Melt the chocolate in a small heatproof bowl over simmering water

for about 4 minutes, stirring, until smooth. Allow to cool slightly after removing from the heat.

2 Utilizing an electric blender fitted with the oar connection, beat the spread, earthy colored sugar, confectioners' sugar, and salt on medium speed for around 3 minutes, or until mixed and smooth. Mix in the peanut butter just until it is incorporated.

3 Use an offset spatula to evenly distribute the mixture into the prepared loaf pan. Press the peanut butter mixture on top of the plastic wrap to make it smooth. Either freeze for 45 to 60 minutes or refrigerate for two to three hours until very cold.

4 Place the candy on a work surface and line it with foil or parchment paper from the loaf pan. After removing the foil or paper, invert the rectangle onto a plate or cutting board. Utilizing a huge blade, trim off the edges to make an even-edged square shape (snack on them — so great). Spread out the melted chocolate all over the top. Put in the refrigerator for two hours until very cold.

5 To serve, cut the candy longwise into two 1½ far reaching strips. Divide each strip into ten segments. Store in a water/air proof compartment in the cooler for as long as 5 days. Always serve at room temperature.

VERSION This recipe also yields an insanely delicious peanut butter s'more. Fill homemade

Cinnamon Graham Crackers with room-temperature peanut butter, then top with another graham, a toasted homemade Marshmallow, and Best-Ever Chocolate Sauce.

red velvet twinks

MAKES 16 Twinkies are one more #1 from my young life, and this recipe makes a comparative bite cake with a southern bend. Several years into my career as a pastry chef, I had my first experience with red velvet. I became familiar with this local favorite while working in Miami quickly, and the classic Twinkie has benefited from my conversion. The traditional cream cheese filling is elevated to a whole new level with goat cheese's wonderful tang.

FOR THE CAKES

2½ cups cake flour

2 tablespoons regular dim cocoa powder (ideally Valrhona)

1 teaspoon legitimate salt

1½ cups sugar

1½ cups canola oil

An additional 2 enormous eggs, at room temperature

2 teaspoons vanilla bean glue or unadulterated vanilla concentrate

1 teaspoon red food shading gel (or 2 teaspoons fluid shading)

1 cup buttermilk, at room temperature

2 teaspoons white vinegar

1½ teaspoons baking pop

FOR THE FILLING

4 ounces cream cheddar, at room temperature

4 ounces goat cheddar, at room temperature

6 tablespoons (¾ stick) unsalted spread, at room temperature

1½ cups confectioners' sugar

1 teaspoon vanilla bean glue or unadulterated vanilla concentrate

½ teaspoon legitimate salt

2 cups hacked toasted walnuts or destroyed coconut

1 To make the cakes, position racks in the upper center and lower center of the stove, and preheat the broiler to 350°F (325°F if utilizing a convection broiler). Delicately oil (ideally with Pam) 2 kayak baking container. (These pans have eight oblong cups with rounded bottoms, just like muffin tins. They can be purchased either in bakeware or gourmet equipment stores or online.)

2 Combine the salt, cocoa powder, and flour by sifting them.

3 Beat the sugar and oil on medium speed with an electric mixer fitted with a whisk attachment until well combined. Add the eggs, vanilla, and food shading and beat on medium speed for 1 moment, until mixed. Beat on low speed after adding a third of the flour mixture until just combined. Mix in half of the buttermilk on low speed just until combined. Continue mixing until the dough just comes together with the remaining flour mixture and buttermilk, ending with the last third of the flour mixture.

4 Mix the vinegar and baking soft drink together in a little bowl. Add to the hitter and mix utilizing an elastic spatula until recently mixed.

5 Divide the batter evenly among the baking pans that have been prepared. Prepare for 17 to 19 minutes (14 to 17 minutes if utilizing a convection stove), exchanging the baking dish's positions part of the way through baking, until the tops feel somewhat firm and a toothpick embedded in the focal point of one cake tells the truth. Allow the

baking pans to cool completely before moving them to wire racks.

6 To make the filling, beat the cream cheese, goat cheese, and butter with a paddle attachment on a medium speed for about 2 minutes until soft and smooth. Beat on medium-high speed for 2 minutes after adding the vanilla, salt, and confectioners' sugar until smooth and fluffy.

7 Transfer three-quarters of the filling to a piping bag with a plain 14-inch tip, leaving the remaining quarter in the bowl for use in the subsequent step.

8 On the grounds that the round top of these cakes really turns into the base, you'll need to manage off this adjusted part utilizing a serrated blade. To fill a cake, hold it flat side up with one hand and insert the pastry bag's tip about an inch from the cake's end into the flat side. Incorporate approximately one tablespoon of the filling into the cake. Rehash 2 additional times, equitably separating the filling across the cake. Cover the bottom with a thin layer of the remaining icing using a small spatula. Place the bottom, rounded side up, on a serving plate after dipping it in coconut or pecans. Rehash with the excess cakes. Serve immediately or keep for up to three days in the refrigerator in an airtight container.

tootses MAKES 24 (2-INCH) ROLLS During my time at the Culinary Institute of America, I learned how to make intricate and out-of-date cake ornaments. I realized that the modeling chocolate I was using tasted exactly like Tootsie Rolls after tasting it. The problem was that I couldn't think of a bride who would want a Tootsie Roll cake. This recipe was the result of some work I did on them. They're not the Tootsies you grew up with yet are way better. I like to serve these enveloped with foil for a retro, charming, and truly simple to-make treat.

7 ounces ambivalent chocolate (ideally Valrhona Caraïbe 66%), cleaved

¼ cup Lyle's Brilliant Syrup (found in most supermarkets)

1 Dissolve the chocolate in a little heatproof bowl set over stewing water, mixing until the chocolate is liquefied and smooth. Eliminate the bowl from the intensity and put away for 3 minutes to marginally cool. The chocolate ought to be around 110°F.

2 Mix in the syrup until recently mixed. Cover the bowl with saran wrap and put away at room temperature for around 60 minutes, or until the candy is firm yet pliable. If you have any desire to speed things along, put the bowl in the cooler and mix each 2 to 3 minutes, watching out for it since it will solidify rapidly.

3 Place the candy on a work surface and divide it into thirds; the portions do not have to be perfectly even. Use your hands to knead the chocolate until it is soft and pliable (similar to Play-Doh), working with one third at a time and covering the remainder with plastic wrap.

4 Roll the chocolate into a 12-inch-long, long rope. Cut the roll into 2-inch-long pieces with a small knife. Wrap them exclusively in foil, treats coverings, or waxed paper. Use the remaining chocolate to repeat. Store the rolls at room temperature for as long as about fourteen days — however I don't think they'll keep going that long.

popcorn + nut bark

MAKES 1 POUND

Bark, thing: Intense defensive covering of the woody stems of trees.

Peanut Bark and popcorn, noun: Heavenly dull chocolate covering safeguarding rich, pungent, newly popped popcorn and peanuts.

Verb bark: Talk in a threatening tone when it's undeniably gone.

12 ounces clashing chocolate, (ideally Valrhona Caraïbe 66%), slashed

3 cups newly popped popcorn

½ cup salted peanuts (ideally Virginia)

Spot of fit salt

1 Line a baking sheet with a nonstick liner.

2 Dissolve the chocolate in an enormous heatproof bowl set over stewing water, mixing until the chocolate is liquefied and smooth, around 4 minutes. Eliminate the bowl from the intensity and add the popcorn, peanuts, and salt. Overlap the combination until the popcorn and peanuts are equitably covered with the chocolate.

3 Scratch the blend onto the pre-arranged baking sheet and spread into a far layer.

4 Place in the refrigerator for about thirty minutes, or until firm and cold. Break into small

clusters and keep in the refrigerator for up to five days in an airtight container.

16 "PIES" of mochaccino whoopie pies are made each summer when my family would drive along Maine's coastline. At the point when I was extremely youthful, we would make this excursion without cooling. Extremely hot. I dreaded having to travel, but the reward at the end of that long, hot trip was worth it all: we'd stop at Labadies' Bread kitchen in Lewiston, Maine (it's been there beginning around 1925), for the most incredibly sweet, light, and feathery whoopie pies.

FOR THE CAKES

2 cups regular flour

½ cup regular dull cocoa powder (ideally Valrhona)

1 tablespoon finely ground coffee beans

½ teaspoon baking pop

1 teaspoon ground cinnamon (ideally Saigon, see note)

½ cup (1 stick) unsalted spread, at room temperature

1 cup (stuffed) dim earthy colored sugar

1 teaspoon legitimate salt

An additional 1 huge egg, at room temperature

1 teaspoon vanilla bean glue or unadulterated vanilla concentrate

1 cup buttermilk (not low-fat), at room temperature

FOR THE FILLING

4 ounces ambivalent chocolate, (ideally Valrhona Caraïbe 66%), finely slashed

2 tablespoons weighty cream

¾ cup (1½ sticks) in addition to 2 tablespoons unsalted spread, at room temperature

An additional 6 huge egg yolks, at room temperature

¾ cup confectioners' sugar

1½ teaspoons vanilla bean glue or unadulterated vanilla concentrate

¼ teaspoon genuine salt

1 To make the cakes, position racks in the upper center and lower center of the stove, and preheat the broiler to 350°F (325°F if utilizing a convection stove). Line 2 baking sheets with material paper or nonstick liners.

2 Combine the flour, baking soda, cinnamon, ground espresso, and cocoa powder by sifting them together.

3 Beat the butter on medium speed for three minutes, or until smooth and soft, with an electric mixer fitted with a paddle attachment. Beat on medium speed for about 5 minutes, adding the salt and sugar, until fluffy. Mix in the vanilla and the egg until well combined. Scratch down the sides of the bowl. Despite the appearance of curdling, I guarantee that everything will come together.

4 Beat a third of the flour mixture in with the mixer on low speed just until combined. Mix in half of the buttermilk on low speed just until combined. Rehash with the second third of the flour combination and the final part of the buttermilk, finishing with the last third of the flour blend, blending until the batter simply meets up.

5 Utilizing a 2-tablespoon frozen yogurt scoop, shape the mixture into balls and orchestrate around 2 inches separated on the pre-arranged

baking sheets. Switching the positions of the baking sheets halfway through baking will allow you to bake the cakes for 10 to 12 minutes, or until a toothpick inserted into the center of one cake comes out clean. Move the baking sheets to totally wire racks and let cool.

6 To make the filling, heat the chocolate, cream, and 2 tablespoons of the butter in a small heatproof bowl over simmering water until the chocolate and butter are melted. Put away and save the stewing water.

7 Utilizing an electric blender fitted with the whisk connection, beat the egg yolks on medium-rapid for around 3 minutes, until they become pale and thick. Add the chocolate combination and beat on medium-fast for 1 moment, until all around mixed. Place the bowl over the stewing water and cook the combination, whisking continually, for 3 minutes or until it is extremely thick.

8 Eliminate the bowl from the intensity and set it in a bowl loaded up with ice and a little water. Until the mixture reaches room temperature, stir occasionally. Add the excess ¾ cup margarine, the confectioners' sugar, vanilla, and salt to the cooled chocolate. Utilizing an electric blender fitted with the whisk connection, beat on medium-high velocity for 2 minutes, or until very much mixed and smooth.

9 Scratch the filling into a cake pack fitted with a ½-inch plain tip. (You can substitute an ice cream scoop with two tablespoons.) On a work surface,

arrange half of the cooled cakes flat side up. Pipe around 2 to 3 tablespoons of filling onto the focal point of each cake. Place the remaining cakes on top, rounded side up, and gently press the filling down to the edges. Keep in a container that keeps out air. The cakes are best consumed the day they are filled, but they can be stored for two to three days.

fig new t's

MAKES 45 Each time I make this recipe, it helps me to remember nursery school break and how the children used to ridicule me for eating Fig Newtons. " Yucky," they would agree when I hauled them out of my lunchbox. I enjoyed them plain and mashed with soft vanilla ice cream in a bowl. I should have known at the time that I had a slightly different palate. I love to eat these with Black Licorice Ice Cream these days. Whirl ⅓ cup of disintegrated New T's into the completed frozen yogurt for a basic sweet.

FOR THE FILLING

1½ cups (stuffed) managed and coarsely slashed dried figs

¾ cup red wine (ideally Merlot)

⅓ cup sugar

¾ teaspoon finely ground lemon zing

¾ teaspoon anise seeds

FOR THE Mixture

½ cup (1 stick) unsalted margarine, at room temperature

½ cup sugar

1 teaspoon vanilla bean glue or unadulterated vanilla concentrate

1 teaspoon finely ground lemon zing

½ teaspoon fit salt

An additional 1 enormous egg, at room temperature

1½ cups regular baking flour

1 To make the filling, in a medium pan, consolidate the figs, red wine, sugar, lemon zing, and anise seeds with 1 cup water. Cook the mixture, stirring occasionally, for approximately 4 minutes over medium heat until it begins to boil. When the combination is bubbling, lessen the intensity to low and stew, blending sporadically, for 50 to 55 minutes or until the natural product is delicate and the fluid is sweet and decreased to

about ½ cup. Put away, mixing at times, until it cools to room temperature.

2 Scratch the cooled filling into a food processor and heartbeat until the combination is smooth. Cover and store in the refrigerator for up to a week before using.

3 To make the dough, beat the butter on medium speed for three minutes, until it is smooth and soft, with an electric mixer fitted with a paddle attachment. Add the sugar, vanilla, lemon zing, and salt and beat on medium high for around 3 minutes, until very much mixed.

4 Beat for one minute before adding the egg. Beat on medium speed until the flour is just incorporated.

5 Orchestrate 2 enormous bits of saran wrap on a work surface. Divide the dough into two equal portions, place them on the plastic, cover, and form each into a flat, even disc. Put in the refrigerator for about one hour, or until it is firm enough to roll out.

6 Place a substantial amount of parchment paper on a work surface. Working with each plate in turn, put the batter on the focal point of the paper and top with one more sheet of material paper. Roll the dough into a rectangle that is slightly larger than 1114 by 15 inches, stopping every so often to remove the paper, lightly flour the dough, and reposition the paper so that there are no wrinkles. Try to keep the rectangle in a neat

shape—this will help ensure that the number of cookies is accurate. Slide the mixture in the material onto a baking sheet and refrigerate for 60 minutes, or until the batter is extremely firm. If you have any desire to chill it quicker, put it in your cooler and chill for 20 minutes.

7 Preheat the oven to 350°F (325°F if using a convection oven), placing racks in the upper middle and lower middle of the oven. Line 2 baking sheets with material paper or nonstick liners.

8 Working with each sheet in turn, slide the mixture onto a work surface and strip away the top piece of material paper. Dust the batter daintily with flour, and reposition the paper so you get no kinks. Peel off the second piece of parchment paper and flip the dough over. Cut the dough into three equal strips along its length with a small knife and a ruler.

9 Pipe the fig filling down the middle of each strip using a pastry bag with a plain tip that is 12 inches long. Fold the dough carefully over the filling and press the edges together with your fingertips (there isn't much dough here). Roll the treat so the crease is on the base. Slice into pieces that are 112 inches wide and arrange them on the baking sheets that have been prepared about 1 inch apart.

10 Prepare for 15 to 17 minutes (12 to 15 minutes if utilizing a convection broiler), exchanging the baking sheets' positions part of the way through baking, until the tops are pale brilliant and the

bottoms are brilliant brown. Move the baking sheets to totally wire racks and let cool.

CHANGES Apricot: Replace the figs with the same amount of chopped dried apricots; substitute a similar measure of finely ground orange zing for the lemon zing in the filling and in the mixture; utilize white wine rather than red; furthermore, use poppy seeds rather than anise seeds.

Alter any other flavor combination and substitute dried cherries, cranberries, or golden raisins in place of some or all of the figs.

18 pieces of chocolate caramel peanut bars are made by Amy, my assistant, who has been working on perfecting the classic Snickers bar. Each new clump of caramel and nut bars she makes draws nearer to the genuine article. Let me change that to: Amy's adaptation rises above the locally acquired ones, making her creation our most famous early lunch thing in the Hedy's Life as a youngster Treats segment of the menu at Michael's Veritable Food and Drink. Amers, thank you for this one!

These are made in two batches, one of which I keep in the freezer. They might even taste better when served frozen, in my opinion. You choose.

8 ounces milk chocolate (ideally Valrhona), hacked

¾ cup sugar

⅓ cup weighty cream, at room temperature

6 ounces white chocolate (ideally Valrhona), hacked

1 teaspoon legitimate salt

1 cup salted peanuts (ideally Virginia)

1 Line the base and sides of a 8½ × 4½-inch portion dish with material paper or foil and oil it gently (ideally with Pam). Soften the milk chocolate in a little heatproof bowl set over stewing water, mixing until the chocolate is liquefied and smooth. Take the bowl off the stove. Pour half of the milk chocolate into the pre-arranged portion dish and spread it equally. Cool down by freezing for 15 to 18 minutes.

2 When the first layer is cold, make the second one. In an enormous pot, join the sugar and ¼ cup water. Cook, stirring frequently, over low heat until the sugar has dissolved and the liquid is clear.

3 Turn the heat up to medium-high and bring the mixture to a boil without stirring for three to five minutes, or until the sugar begins to turn golden brown on the edges. While tenderly and consistently whirling the container over the

intensity to level out the variety, cook for 2 to 3 minutes, or until the sugar becomes a striking shade of golden.

4 Slide the container from the intensity and gradually add the cream. Careful! It will splatter up, and the steam is hot. Mix until all around mixed. Stir in the salt and white chocolate until the chocolate melts and the mixture is smooth. Mix in the peanuts by adding them and stirring. Put away for 5 minutes to somewhat cool.

5 Evenly distribute the peanut mixture over the milk chocolate in the loaf pan. Freeze for around 45 minutes, or until cold and firm.

6 When the first layer is cold, make the second one. Warm the excess milk chocolate, pour it over the caramel, and spread it uniformly. Refrigerate or freeze for 20 to 30 minutes, until freezing.

7 Utilizing the material paper or foil dish liner, move the candy onto a work surface. Strip away the paper or foil, and put the sweets on a cutting board. Utilizing a huge blade, trim off the edges and cut longwise into two 1½ all inclusive strips. Divide each strip into nine parts. Store in a water/air proof compartment in the cooler for as long as 5 days.

Variation: Blend some of the Chocolate Caramel Peanut Bars, any flavor of ice cream, some milk, and some malted milk powder in a blender to make an amazing milkshake. Gracious no doubt! Throw in a banana, and guarantee it's "solid."

Milk chocolate bunnies, cream-filled Easter eggs, and salty, peanut-flavored candy bars filled my childhood. milk chocolate candy bars MAKES 18 PIECES For my "grown-up" variant of a work of art, I consolidate all my #1 flavors and surfaces into one nibble of wanton sentimentality.

For the first layer, use 12 ounces chopped gianduja (Italian hazelnut milk chocolate) or milk chocolate (preferably Valrhona) and 2 teaspoons canola oil. For the second layer, use 5 ounces bittersweet chocolate (preferably Valrhona Carabe 66%) and chop 12 ounces of heavy cream. For the third layer, use 6 ounces bittersweet chocolate (preferably Valrhona Carabe 66%) and chop 1 ounce

2 To make the primary layer, in a medium heatproof bowl set over stewing water, liquefy the gianduja or milk chocolate. Add the canola oil and the peanut butter and mix until very much mixed and smooth. If this mixture isn't very hot and doesn't burn, it won't cut into nice slices. Add the squashed treats or cereal and the peanuts, and mix until mixed.

3 Use an offset spatula to evenly distribute the mixture into the prepared loaf pan. Press the plastic wrap against the chocolate to smooth the top. Freeze or refrigerate for one to three hours, or until extremely cold.

4 Once the layer is cold, make the subsequent layer. Melt the bittersweet chocolate in a small heatproof bowl set over simmering water. Stir in the heavy cream until it is well combined and

smooth. Allow to cool to room temperature and set aside.

5 Eliminate the plastic from the portion container and scratch the ambivalent blend into the dish over the principal layer. Utilizing an offset spatula, spread it uniformly. Press the plastic wrap against the chocolate to smooth the top. Refrigerate for 1 to 2 hours or until freezing.

6 Once the subsequent layer is cold, make the third layer. Melt the bittersweet chocolate in a small heatproof bowl set over simmering water. Keeping the chocolate exceptionally warm over the water is critical. Utilizing an electric blender fitted with the whisk connection, beat the cream on medium-fast until delicate pinnacles hold when the mixer is lifted. Beat on medium speed for about one minute after adding the very warm chocolate until well blended and very thick.

7 Scrape the chocolate-and-whipped cream mixture into the loaf pan over the second layer after removing the plastic. Utilizing an offset spatula, spread it uniformly. Press the plastic wrap against the chocolate to smooth the top. Refrigerate the loaf pan in its entirety in a plastic wrap for two to four hours, or up to three days.

8 To serve, transfer the candy to a work surface using the foil liner or parchment paper. Strip away the paper or foil, and put the sweets on a cutting board. Filter the cocoa powder equally beyond absurd. Utilizing a huge blade dunked in steaming hot water and cleaned dry, trim off the edges. Slice the candy into 34-inch-wide slices by dipping the

knife in hot water and wiping it dry between cuts. Store in a hermetically sealed holder in the cooler for 3 to 4 days

marshmallows

MAKES 40 (1½-INCH) MARSHMALLOWS What kind of stream do they use to "fly puff" those locally acquired marshmallows, at any rate? Hand crafted marshmallows are a disclosure to the people who have just had the grocery store assortments. While marshmallows help me to remember lounging around a pit fire at day camp, my straightforward recipe is extraordinary all year and for all events — without the need to sort out some way to land a 747 in your kitchen for that "fly puffed" impact.

13 cup cornstarch 13 cup confectioners' sugar 22 cup unflavored powdered gelatin 24 cup granulated sugar 14 teaspoon Lyle's Golden Syrup (available in most supermarkets) 2 large, room-temperature egg whites 14 teaspoon vanilla bean paste or pure vanilla extract 1 In a medium bowl, sift the confectioners' sugar and whisk it together. Sprinkle a third of the mixture evenly over the bottom of a baking dish measuring 9 x 13 inches.

2 In a little pot, sprinkle the gelatin over ¾ cup water and put away for 3 minutes, or until the gelatin has mellowed and sprouted. Warm for about two minutes over low heat, stirring frequently, until the gelatin is dissolved and the

liquid is clear but not boiling. Eliminate from the intensity.

3 In a little pot, join ¾ cup water with the granulated sugar and syrup. Cook over low intensity, blending sometimes, until the sugar is broken up and the fluid is clear, around 3 to 5 minutes. Place a candy thermometer on the pan's side and turn the heat up to medium-high. For three to five minutes, cook the syrup without stirring until it reaches 260°F.

4 Meanwhile, beat the egg whites with an electric mixer fitted with a whisk attachment until they form medium-soft peaks, about 2 minutes, or until the sugar reaches 240 degrees Fahrenheit.

5 When the sugar syrup comes to 260°F, slide the skillet from the intensity and add the broke up gelatin and the vanilla. Stir to combine.

6 With the blender on medium-high velocity, gradually pour the hot sugar syrup down the side of the bowl of egg whites. Beat the whites for another six minutes, or until they are just slightly warm and cool.

7 Scratch the marshmallow into the pre-arranged baking dish and spread it equitably. Perform this step immediately because the gelatin will quickly cool, making it difficult to spread.

8 Filter one more third of the cornstarch and confectioners' sugar combination equitably over the marshmallow. For approximately four hours,

or until the marshmallow is very firm, place the dish at room temperature.

9 Run a little blade around the edge of the marshmallow and modify it onto a work surface. Utilizing an enormous blade, cut the marshmallow transversely into eight 1½ far reaching strips. Cut each strip into 5 squares and throw with the leftover cornstarch and confectioners' sugar combination. Store in a hermetically sealed compartment for as long as 5 days.

Variations: Substitute one of the pure extracts listed below for the vanilla with one-half teaspoon: coconut, almond, or maple.

Likewise, I like to add 3 tablespoons of cocoa nibs (see note) to the marshmallow just prior to eliminating it from the blender. The chocolatey morsels are delectable!

BROWNIES

coconut macadamia bites MAKE 36 PIECES These tropical bites are packed with a lot of powerful flavors thanks to the buttery, crunchy macadamia nuts and rich coconut. Envision walnut pie goes on a tropical excursion and returns home murmuring Sway Marley tunes.

Serve these by themselves or in the current style alongside Rum Toffee Sauce and Truly Extraordinary Vanilla Frozen yogurt.

FOR THE Outside layer

¾ cup (1½ sticks) unsalted spread, at room temperature

½ cup granulated sugar

Touch of fit salt

An additional 1 huge egg yolk, at room temperature

¼ teaspoon vanilla bean glue or unadulterated vanilla concentrate

2⅓ cups cake flour, filtered

FOR THE FILLING

1 cup (2 sticks) unsalted spread, cut into 6 pieces

1 cup (stuffed) dim earthy colored sugar

¼ cup granulated sugar

¾ cup honey (ideally natural and nearby)

1 pound macadamia nuts, coarsely hacked and toasted

½ cup improved destroyed coconut

¼ cup weighty cream, at room temperature

½ teaspoon vanilla bean glue or unadulterated vanilla concentrate

Spot of legitimate salt

1 To make the covering, line the base and sides a 9 × 13-inch baking dish with material paper or foil and oil it daintily (ideally with Pam).

2 Beat the butter for about three minutes on medium speed with an electric mixer fitted with a paddle attachment, until it is smooth and soft. Beat for about three minutes on medium-high speed after adding the salt and granulated sugar. Add the egg yolk and vanilla and beat for 1 moment, or until very much mixed. Beat on medium speed until the flour is just incorporated.

3 Scratch the batter into the pre-arranged baking dish. Plunge your fingers in flour and press the batter into an even layer to cover the lower part of the skillet, redipping in flour on a case by case basis to hold things back from being excessively tacky. Prick the crust all over with a fork's tines. Chill for 15 minutes in the refrigerator.

4 Preheat the oven to 350°F (325°F if using a convection oven) by placing a rack in the center.

5 Heat for 20 to 22 minutes (18 to 20 minutes if utilizing a convection stove), until the hull is pale brilliant. While you prepare the filling, transfer the baking pan to a wire rack to cool. Keep the broiler set to 350°F (325°F if utilizing a convection stove).

6 To make the filling, melt the butter in a large saucepan over low heat for about 2 minutes, stirring frequently. Honey, granulated sugar, and brown sugar should be added. Cook, stirring occasionally, over medium-high heat until the mixture reaches a boil. Stop stirring the mixture once it reaches a boil and cook for three minutes.

7 Slide the container from the intensity, and add the macadamia nuts, coconut, cream, vanilla, and salt. Combine with a mixer. Pour the filling over the hull and spread it into an even layer.

8 Heat for 24 to 26 minutes (20 to 24 minutes if utilizing a convection broiler), until the filling is percolating and profound brown. It will still appear to be very wet and soft, but it will harden as it cools.

9 Allow the baking dish to cool completely (overnight is preferred) on a wire rack.

10 Remove the cookie from the pan and place it on a cutting board using the foil or parchment liner before serving. Strip away the foil or paper, and utilizing an enormous blade, cut the treat the long

way into 3 long strips, then, at that point, cut each strip into 12 equivalent pieces. For up to a week, store in an airtight container.

S'more brownies yield 12 brownies My very first batch came from a ready-to-use mix. I was six years of age and couldn't hold on to try out my Simple Heat Stove. I painstakingly followed the bearings bit by bit. I read and rehash each line again and again. I trusted in the enchantment of that sixty-watt bulb that heated my brownie to fudgy flawlessness. I'm still that six-year-old who thinks anything is possible in some ways. This brownie is evidence that wizardry occurs, particularly when you join chocolate and custom made marshmallows and graham saltines.

8 ounces mixed chocolate (ideally Valrhona Caraïbe 66%), cleaved

½ cup (1 stick) unsalted spread, cut into 6 pieces

¾ cup sugar

½ cup regular flour

¼ teaspoon baking powder

½ teaspoon legitimate salt

An additional 2 huge eggs, at room temperature

⅓ cup sharp cream, at room temperature

2 teaspoons vanilla bean glue or unadulterated vanilla concentrate

1 cup graham wafer pieces (ideally custom made)

8 huge marshmallows (ideally custom made)

½ cup semisweet or mixed chocolate chips (ideally Valrhona)

1 Position a rack in the focal point of the stove, and preheat the broiler to 350°F (325°F if utilizing a convection broiler). Grease an 8-inch square baking dish that has been lined with parchment or foil (Pam is preferred).

2 Melt the butter and chocolate in a small heatproof bowl over simmering water. Rush until smooth, and put away to marginally cool.

3 Whisk together the sugar, flour, baking powder, and salt in a medium bowl.

4 Whisk the eggs, sour cream, and vanilla in a large bowl. Whisk in the flour mixture before adding it. Stir in the melted chocolate until well combined. Stir in the chocolate chips,

marshmallows, and graham crackers gently to combine.

5 Spread the batter as evenly as you can into the baking dish you've prepared. The graham crackers, marshmallows, and chocolate chips will make the top look lumpy. Prepare for 24 to 26 minutes (18 to 19 minutes if utilizing a convection stove), until puffed the middle actually wiggles when the skillet is delicately shaken. (I think these brownies are at their best when marginally underbaked.)

6 Let the baking dish cool completely on a wire rack before placing it in the refrigerator for two hours, or until it is cold and firm. Cut the cool brownie into 12 pieces and store in a hermetically sealed compartment in the fridge for as long as 5 days.

Peanut butter fudge brownies yield 12 brownies when made for my Girl Scout troop in the past. They should have earned me a merit badge because they were always popular! I actually love to prepare a cluster to take to barbecues or gatherings.

8 ounces chopped bittersweet chocolate (preferably Valrhona Carabe 66%), 1 stick unsalted butter, room temperature, 1 cup sugar, 1 cup all-purpose flour, 1 teaspoon baking powder, 1 teaspoon kosher salt, 2 large eggs, room temperature, 1 cup sour cream, room temperature, 1 teaspoon vanilla bean paste or pure vanilla extract, 1 cup, and 2 tablespoons creamy peanut butter (preferably organic), room temperature Line a 8-inch square baking dish with material paper or foil and oil it (ideally with Pam).

2 Melt the butter and chocolate in a small heatproof bowl over simmering water. Whisk until smooth, then set aside for a moment to cool down.

3 In a medium bowl, join the sugar, flour, baking powder, and salt and speed until mixed.

4 Whisk the eggs, sour cream, and vanilla in a large bowl. Whisk in the flour mixture before adding it. Stir in the melted butter and chocolate until well combined. Mix in the peanut butter, 2 tablespoons at a time, until well combined.

5 Evenly distribute the batter into the baking dish that has been prepared. Sprinkle the batter evenly with small blobs of the remaining 1/3 cup of peanut butter. Swirl the peanut butter into the brownie batter with a table knife before smoothing the top.

6 Bake for 40 to 44 minutes (or 30 to 34 if using a convection oven), or until the center still jiggles

when gently shaken. I think these brownies are at their best when marginally underbaked.)

7 Exchange the baking dish to a wire rack and let cool totally prior to refrigerating for 2 hours, or until cold and firm. Cut the cool brownie into 12 pieces and store in a hermetically sealed compartment in the fridge for as long as 5 days.

flavored chocolate pistachio almond baklava

MAKES 36 PIECES There are numerous varieties of baklava, and this is one of my top choices to serve for Rosh Hashanah as a sweet beginning for another year. The flavors are not quite the same as what you'd expect with an exemplary baklava, and the chocolate adds a hint of extravagance. You can try it with a variety of nuts, including walnuts, and flavorings like lavender, ground fennel, and anise seed. Anything will do!

FOR THE BAKLAVA

2 cups pistachios

1 cup entire, unblanched almonds

¾ cup sugar

2 teaspoons ground cinnamon (ideally Saigon, see note)

¼ teaspoon ground cloves

⅛ teaspoon ground cardamom

Squeeze or a greater amount of cayenne pepper

Spot of genuine salt

6 ounces clashing chocolate (ideally Valrhona Caraïbe 66%), coarsely cleaved

1 (16-ounce) bundle frozen phyllo mixture, defrosted

1½ cups (3 sticks) unsalted margarine, liquefied

FOR THE SYRUP

2 cups sugar

1 cup honey (ideally natural and neighborhood)

½ cup new squeezed orange

3 tablespoons finely ground orange zing

1 tablespoon cardamom cases, gently squashed and restricted in cheesecloth

1 To make the baklava, join the pistachios, almonds, sugar, cinnamon, cloves, cardamom,

cayenne, and salt in a food processor. Until the nuts are finely chopped but not ground, pulse five to six times. Scratch into a bowl.

2 Place the chopped chocolate in the food processor without cleaning it and pulse five to six times until the chocolate is the same size as the nuts. Be mindful so as not to overprocess, as it can liquefy the chocolate. Add the chocolate to the nut combination and mix until mixed.

3 Lay the phyllo dough sheets out on a work surface. Trim the sheets to 9 x 13 inches with a large knife and a ruler. To stop the sheets from drying out, wrap them in plastic wrap and cover them with damp paper towels.

4 Butter the bottom and sides of a 9 x 13-inch baking pan lightly with a pastry brush. Smooth out any air bubbles by placing one sheet of phyllo in the pan's bottom. Gently yet completely brush the phyllo with liquefied spread. Butter each layer of the remaining five sheets of phyllo as you go. Spread a third of the nut mixture evenly over the phyllo with your hands.

5 Recurrent the layering with one more 4 sheets of phyllo and margarine. Spread one more third of the nut blend over the mixture.

6 Spread the remaining nut mixture on top of the four additional sheets of buttered phyllo.

7 Butter each of the remaining six phyllo sheets before placing them on top. Cover firmly with cling wrap and refrigerate for 2 hours.

8 Position a rack in the focal point of the broiler, and preheat the stove to 350°F (325°F if utilizing a convection stove).

9 Generally, baklava is cut into triangle-formed pieces, yet I like to cut it into long rectangular pieces. Utilizing a sharp blade, cut the baklava longwise into 3 strips, and afterward cut each strip into 12 pieces. To ensure that the syrup can penetrate the layers, make sure to cut all the way through to the bottom. Bake until golden brown, about one hour. Move the dish to a wire rack.

10 In the mean time, in a medium pan, consolidate the sugar, honey, squeezed orange, orange zing, the cardamom in its cheesecloth, and 1 cup water and heat to the point of boiling, mixing to break up the sugar. Boil for fifteen minutes, or until slightly reduced and thickened. There will be about three cups. Dispose of the cardamom and pour the hot syrup equitably over the baklava. Let cool totally.

11 Retrace the baklava's cuts with a sharp knife, making sure to cut all the way through to the bottom. There will be a little syrup staying at the lower part of the dish. After cooling, serve immediately or cover and store in the refrigerator for up to three days. The baklava cuts best when chilled for the time being.

sugar coated ginger, blackberry + almond rugelach

Causes 32 PIECES Rugelach to have profound roots in Jewish families, and they are the most celebrated little baked good of my young life. They, in my opinion, have the capacity to unite individuals and families. Ask any bubbe (a Jewish grandma) and she will let you know that her "ruggies" are awesome — and you better trust her! Never disagree with a bubba, but do try my recipe. My combination of blackberry jam and candied ginger is a real treat, despite being unusual.

Because it is the best crystallized ginger in the world, I recommend Australian ginger. Made with new child ginger roots, it is delicate, soggy, and exceptionally delightful.

1 cup whole natural almonds, lightly toasted 3 tablespoons sugar 1 teaspoon ground cinnamon (preferably Saigon, see note) 1 teaspoon ground ginger 1 cup coarsely chopped crystallized ginger (preferably Australian) 1 extra-large egg 1 tablespoon whole milk 3 tablespoons sugar 1 teaspoon ground cinnamon (preferably Saigon, see note) 2/3 cup seedless blackberry jam or Pop Jam 1 Beat on medium-high speed for approximately 2 minutes, adding the sugar, lemon zest, vanilla, and salt. Scratch down the sides of the bowl. Mix on low speed until the dough just comes together after adding the flour.

2 Divide the dough in half and scrape it onto a work surface. Wrap each half in plastic wrap to form a flat disc. Put in the refrigerator for about one hour, or until it is firm enough to roll out.

3 To make the filling, join the almonds, sugar, cinnamon, and ground ginger in a food processor. Pulse the nuts until they are coarsely chopped. Pulse in the ginger crystals until they are finely ground.

4 Position a rack in the focal point of the stove, and preheat the broiler to 350°F (325°F if utilizing a convection stove). Line 2 baking sheets with material paper or nonstick liners.

5 Whisk together the milk and egg in a small bowl until well combined. This egg wash can be applied to the rugelach just before baking.

6 In a different little bowl, consolidate the sugar and cinnamon and blend until mixed.

7 Place a substantial amount of parchment paper on a work surface. Working with each circle in turn, put the batter on the focal point of the paper and top the mixture with one more sheet of material paper. Roll the dough into a 12-inch circle, stopping every now and then to remove the paper, lightly dust the dough with flour, and reposition the paper so that there are no wrinkles.

8 Spread half of the jam evenly over the dough with a small offset spatula, leaving a 12-inch border around the edge. Dissipate half of the nut

combination equitably over the jam. Press down hard on the nuts with your hands to ensure that they stay put. Cut the circle into 16 triangles with a pizza wheel or chef's knife.

9 Roll up each triangle starting at the wide end. They will seem to be scaled down croissants. On one of the baking sheets that have been prepared, arrange the cookies with the center tips tucked underneath about an inch apart. Gently brush the highest points of the rugelach with the egg wash and sprinkle with the cinnamon sugar.

10 Bake until golden brown, 35 to 38 minutes (or 30 to 35 minutes if using a convection oven). The cookies should cool completely before moving to a wire rack.

11 Continue with the remaining dough while the first batch is baking. Ruggies that have been baked and chilled can be covered and kept at room temperature for up to three days.

Pistachio, apricot, and cardamom: For the filling, substitute the same amount of toasted pistachios for the toasted almonds and the same amount of ground cardamom for the ground ginger. In place of the blackberry, use an equal amount of apricot jam.

Cherry and Walnut, Chocolate Chip: For the filling, substitute ⅓ cup gently toasted pecans, ¼ cup hacked chocolate, ¼ cup dried cherries, ¼ cup sugar, 1 teaspoon cocoa powder (ideally Valrhona), and ¼ teaspoon ground cinnamon and heartbeat in a food processor until finely slashed. Substitute an equivalent measure of cherry jam for the blackberry.

salted peanut brittle my way MAKES 1 pound I developed this brittle recipe after experiencing difficulties when making brittle in South Florida's high humidity. It's not conventional using any and all means — you could never mix bubbling caramel for dread it would solidify and get sandy when it cools. My rendition doesn't get tacky, stays dry for quite a long time (assuming it endures that long), and it won't adhere to your teeth. This brittle has a significant cult following among me. Be on the lookout, because you won't know it until you start getting calls in the middle of the night asking for a weak "fix."

1½ cups sugar

2 cups salted peanuts (ideally Virginia)

1 tablespoon fleur de sel or other coarse ocean salt

1 Line a baking sheet with a nonstick liner (material paper won't work for weak). Use Pam instead of butter to lubricate the bottom of an offset metal spatula.

2 In a huge pot, join the sugar and 1¼ cups water. Cook, stirring frequently, over low heat until the sugar has dissolved and the liquid is clear. Increment the intensity to medium high, and heat the fluid to the point of boiling.

3 Add the peanuts and cook, stirring frequently, until the edges of the liquid begin to turn a light amber color. The fluid will look dark, not satisfactory like customary brittles or caramel.) The caramel should be a deep amber in color after another 4 to 6 minutes of cooking and stirring to even it out.

4 Cautiously and immediately pour the fragile onto the pre-arranged baking sheet, and utilizing the lubed spatula, spread it into an even layer that is about ½ inch thick. Sprinkle with the fleur de sel. Reminder: Be careful because this caramel stuff is very hot!

5 Allow the brittle to cool completely and harden for about one hour at room temperature. Depending on how hungry you are, break the brittle into small or large pieces and store them in an airtight container for up to five days.

old-school raspberry bars

MAKES 24 BARS These folks are so simple and simple to make that I truly want to believe that they don't get disregarded by the accomplished cook. They are an excellent platform for showcasing a Grapefruit Marmalade or Pop Jam that has won a prize.

An assistant of mine taught me years ago how her grandmother used a box grater to evenly distribute the dough. Yes, unique. These bars get their light and airy texture from grating the dough. However, be careful with your knuckles!

3 cups regular baking flour

1½ teaspoons baking powder

1½ teaspoons fit salt

1½ cups (3 sticks) unsalted margarine, at room temperature

1½ cups granulated sugar

2 teaspoons vanilla bean glue or unadulterated vanilla concentrate

2 teaspoons finely ground lemon zing

An additional 3 enormous egg yolks, at room temperature

1⅓ cups raspberry Pop Jam (or utilize great locally acquired)

⅓ cup confectioners' sugar, for tidying

1 To make the outside layer, filter together the flour, baking powder, and salt.

2 Beat the butter on a medium speed with an electric mixer fitted with a paddle attachment for about three minutes, or until it is smooth and soft. Add the granulated sugar, vanilla, and lemon zing and beat on medium-high velocity for around 2 minutes, until very much mixed. Add the egg yolks, each in turn, and beat for 1 moment or until all around mixed. Beat on medium speed until the flour mixture is just combined.

3 Scratch the mixture and any leftover floury pieces onto a work surface and manipulate 3 to multiple times, until everything meets up into a smooth batter.

4 Gap the batter fifty (gauge the parts on the off chance that you have a scale), shape into logs, and envelop by cling wrap. Freeze the logs for 2 hours, or until extremely firm.

5 Preheat the oven to 350°F (325°F if using a convection oven) by placing a rack in the center. Grease a 9-inch square baking pan lightly (preferably with Pam) and line the bottom and sides with parchment paper or foil.

6 Place a large box grater on a plate, and use the large holes to shred one of the logs; freeze the other. Make sure not to press on the dough pieces as you distribute them evenly throughout the

baking pan that has been prepared. The layers should be soft and fluffy.) Utilizing a little counterbalanced spatula, spread the jam uniformly over the mixture without pushing down on the batter. Shred the leftover log and dissipate the pieces uniformly over the jam. It will be very full in the pan.

7 Heat for 54 to 56 minutes (40 to 45 minutes if utilizing a convection stove), until the top is somewhat puffed and uniformly cooked. Move the baking dish to a wire rack and let cool totally.

8 To serve, utilize the foil or material paper liner to lift the treat from the skillet and onto a cutting board. Strip away the foil or paper, and utilizing a huge blade, cut the treat into 4 strips. Dust each strip with confectioners' sugar after cutting it into six equal pieces. For up to a week, store in an airtight container.

Utilizing a crate grater to shred this batter is an incredible exercise for your lower arms. All things considered, in the event that you're not into the exercise, you can shred the mixture in a food processor — simply make certain to shape the batter into a long log that will squeeze into your processor's taking care of cylinder. Likewise, make certain to work just with exceptionally frozen batter.

This is the Italian trifecta of desserts—a cross between fruitcake, candy, and honey cake—and it makes 36 servings. I prefer to serve panforte (pronounced "pahn-FOR-teh") as bars rather than in a circular pan. After letting the honey and spices combine for a few days, you'll notice that these taste better. Make this the new "nut cake" for occasion gifts. It's a lot cooler and is delectable presented with coffee or affogato, or close by gelato.

2 (8-inch) squares rice paper

1½ cups regular flour

¼ cup regular dull cocoa powder (ideally Valrhona)

1 teaspoon ground cinnamon (ideally Saigon, see note)

¼ teaspoon ground allspice

¼ teaspoon ground cloves

¼ teaspoon ground ginger

1 cup sugar

1 cup honey (ideally natural and nearby)

1 cup hazelnuts, toasted and coarsely hacked

1 cup entire regular almonds, toasted and coarsely cleaved

1 cup (stuffed) coarsely hacked dried apricots

1 Position a rack in the focal point of the stove, and preheat the broiler to 325°F (300°F if utilizing a convection stove). Grease generously (preferably with Pam) the sides of an 8-inch square baking pan. One sheet of rice paper should cover the bottom.

2 In a medium bowl, filter together the flour, cocoa, cinnamon, allspice, cloves, and ginger.

3 In a huge pot, consolidate the sugar and honey. Over medium heat, cook, stirring occasionally, until the mixture reaches a boil. When the mixture reaches a boil, stop stirring and let it cook until a candy thermometer reads 238 to 240 degrees Fahrenheit.

4 Slide the skillet from the intensity and add the flour combination, hazelnuts, almonds, and apricots. Mix until all around mixed.

5 Working rapidly, scratch the combination into the pre-arranged container and spread it into an even layer. Top with the leftover piece of rice paper. Utilizing an offset spatula, press immovably on the paper to make an even layer.

6 Bake for 28 to 30 minutes, or 21 to 22 minutes if using a convection oven, or until the filling is

slightly bubbling at the edges. It will still appear to be very wet and soft, but it will harden as it cools. Place the baking pan on a wire rack and allow it to cool completely (preferably overnight).

7 To serve, run a blade around the edge of the dish and upset onto a cutting board. Utilizing a huge blade, cut the panforte into 3 strips and cut each strip into 12 equivalent pieces. For up to a week, store in an airtight container.

COOKIES/BISCUITS

mexican "hot cocoa" wedding treats

MAKES 27 Treats Cinco de Mayo is my number one occasion, and I celebrate it with energy. I worked for a long time as a cake gourmet specialist at Imprint's Place in North Miami. Mark

Militello, the culinary expert and proprietor, had a similar love of this occasion. Each May 4 and 5, we would change the menu completely to a valid Mexican subject. The champion recipe for me was this astounding little treat, which is jam-loaded with flavor. My chocolate wedding treats have a kick of flavor and are so natural to make.

1¼ cups regular flour

½ cup regular dull cocoa powder (ideally Valrhona)

1 teaspoon ground cinnamon (ideally Saigon, see note)

1 teaspoon finely ground coffee beans

½ teaspoon ground allspice

¼ teaspoon ground cloves

¼ teaspoon ground chipotle bean stew pepper

10 tablespoons (1¼ sticks) unsalted margarine, at room temperature

¾ cup (pressed) dull earthy colored sugar

2 teaspoons finely ground orange zing

¾ teaspoon fit salt

1 teaspoon vanilla bean glue or unadulterated vanilla concentrate

Confectioners' sugar, for serving

1 Position racks in the upper center and lower center of the broiler, and preheat the stove to 325°F (300°F if utilizing a convection stove). Line 2 baking sheets with material paper or nonstick liners.

2 Filter together the flour, cocoa powder, cinnamon, ground coffee, allspice, cloves, and chipotle powder.

3 Utilizing an electric blender fitted with the oar connection, beat the margarine on medium speed for around 3 minutes, until delicate and smooth. Add the earthy colored sugar, orange zing, and salt and beat on medium-fast for around 5 minutes, until light and soft. Add the vanilla and blend until mixed. Scratch down the sides of the bowl. Add the flour combination and beat on low speed until the mixture simply meets up.

4 Utilizing a 1-tablespoon frozen yogurt scoop, shape the batter into balls and organize them around 1½ inches separated on the pre-arranged baking sheets. Prepare for 14 to 16 minutes (8 to 10 minutes if utilizing a convection broiler), exchanging the baking sheets' positions part of the way through baking, until the tops feel somewhat firm and the flavors are extremely fragrant. Move the baking sheets to wire racks and let the treats cool totally.

5 Store in a sealed shut compartment for as long as 5 days. Dust with just the right amount of confectioners' sugar prior to serving.

garbage in da trunk

MAKES 16 (2½-INCH) Treats Might a treat at any point characterize a vocation? Indeed, this is THAT treat. Throughout the long term, the recipe has remained fundamentally something very similar — consistently gooey, pungent, and astonishing — with the supporting players changing relying upon where my head is on a given day. I've added everything to this player from peppermint patties to nut weak to peanut butter to stuffed pretzels. Be imaginative!

1¾ cups regular flour

¾ teaspoon baking pop

½ cup (1 stick) unsalted spread, at room temperature

½ cup (stuffed) dim earthy colored sugar

½ cup granulated sugar

¾ teaspoon genuine salt

An additional 1 huge egg, at room temperature

1 teaspoon vanilla bean glue or unadulterated vanilla concentrate

6 ounces ambivalent chocolate (ideally Valrhona 70%), cut into ½-inch pieces

⅓ cup daintily squashed pot cooked potato chips

⅓ cup coarsely cleaved salted pretzels

⅓ cup butterscotch pieces

12 malted milk balls, cut down the middle (about ⅓ cup)

⅓ cup salted peanuts (ideally Virginia), coarsely slashed

Coarse ocean salt, for sprinkling

1 Filter together the flour and baking pop.

2 Utilizing an electric blender fitted with the oar connection, beat the margarine on medium speed for around 3 minutes, until delicate and smooth. Add the earthy colored sugar, granulated sugar, and salt and beat on medium-rapid for 5 minutes, until light and cushioned. Scratch down the sides of the bowl.

3 Add the egg and vanilla and beat for 1 to 2 minutes, until recently mixed. Add the flour blend and beat on low speed until recently consolidated. Don't overmix.

4 Utilizing an elastic spatula, scratch down the sides of the bowl. Add the chocolate, potato chips, pretzels, butterscotch pieces, malted milk balls, and peanuts. Mix until recently mixed. Try not to be concerned assuming it appears as though there is more garbage than treat batter.

5 Utilizing a 3-tablespoon frozen yogurt scoop, shape the batter into balls and organize them near one another on an enormous plate or little baking sheet.

6 Cover and refrigerate for no less than 60 minutes, until all around chilled. The batter can likewise be covered and refrigerated for the time being, or as long as 2 days prior to baking. Update: Cold mixture heats better.

7 Position the stove racks in the upper center and lower center of the broiler, and preheat the stove to 350°F (335°F if utilizing a convection broiler). Line 2 baking sheets with material paper or nonstick liners. Orchestrate the chilled mixture balls around 2 inches separated on the pre-arranged baking sheets. Utilizing the center of your hand, smooth every batter ball somewhat. Sprinkle the tops with a touch of ocean salt.

8 Heat for 11 to 13 minutes (8 to 9 minutes if utilizing a convection stove), exchanging the baking sheets' positions partially through baking, until light brilliant brown. I think these treats are at their best when somewhat underbaked and the chocolate looks sloppy and gooey. Move the baking sheets to wire racks and let the treats cool

totally. Store in a water/air proof compartment for as long as 5 days and warm prior to serving.

cinnamon graham wafers

MAKES 30 Treats For those of you not acquainted with this storm inclined, promontory molded place alluded to as the Daylight State, key lime pie rules, and graham saltines assume a significant supporting part. (If you have any desire to taste quite possibly of the most ideal adaptation in Miami, simply head over to Joe's Stone Crab.) Throughout the long term, I have made many key lime pastries and have fostered this extraordinary graham wafer recipe. Heat a portion of these children, and I guarantee you won't buy locally acquired grahams once more. Correct, simple for me to say (I'm a cake cook), yet this recipe is really basic and flavorful.

1¼ cups regular baking flour

1 cup entire wheat flour

½ teaspoon baking powder

4 teaspoons ground cinnamon (ideally Saigon, see note)

½ teaspoon newly ground nutmeg

Spot of ground cloves

¾ cup (1½ sticks) unsalted margarine, at room temperature

⅓ cup (pressed) dull earthy colored sugar

5 tablespoons granulated sugar

1 tablespoon honey (ideally natural and neighborhood)

1 tablespoon molasses

½ teaspoon fit salt

An additional 1 enormous egg, at room temperature

1 teaspoon vanilla bean glue or unadulterated vanilla concentrate

1 Filter together the flours, baking powder, 2 teaspoons of the cinnamon, the nutmeg, and the cloves.

2 Utilizing an electric blender fitted with the oar connection, beat the margarine on medium speed for around 3 minutes, until delicate and smooth.

3 Add the earthy colored sugar, 3 tablespoons of the granulated sugar, the honey, molasses, and salt and beat on medium-fast for 5 minutes, until light and soft.

anise almond biscotti

MAKES 20 TO 24 BISCOTTI Working with sugar the entire day, consistently, causes me to acknowledge how much sugar I consume consistently, so I attempt to restrict my admission. Having said that, anise biscotti are my shortcoming. These are basic, rich, and clear. They consolidate my #1 flavors (anise notes, almonds), have a crunchy surface, and are not excessively sweet. Straightforward, without a doubt, I love this biscotti.

1½ cups regular flour

1 teaspoon baking powder

¼ teaspoon legitimate salt

1 cup sugar

3 tablespoons entire anise seeds

1½ cups entire regular almonds

CUSTARDS

tangerine creamsicle pots de crème

SERVES 6 The Orange Julius was a hit at the 1964 New York World's Fair. Who would have thought that milk, vanilla, and orange juice could be so delicious? When I was a kid, It blew my mind, and ever since, I've been pondering the ideal vehicle for the flavors. My tribute to that fantastic combination is this recipe.

1 1/2 cups heavy cream 1 split vanilla bean (see note) 1 tablespoon finely grated tangerine zest 1 pinch of kosher salt 6 large egg yolks 1 1/2 cups sugar 1 1/2 cups fresh tangerine juice 1 Scratch every one of the seeds from the vanilla bean, and add them to the pan alongside the bean, the tangerine zing, and salt. Approximately four minutes, cook over medium heat until very warm but not boiling.

2 Cover the pan, set it aside for at least 30 minutes, and turn off the heat.

3 Preheat the oven to 300°F (275°F if using a convection oven) by placing a rack in the middle of the oven.

4 Place six 6-ounce ramekins in a baking pan with sides that are 2 inches high.

5 Whisk the sugar and egg yolks in a medium bowl until well combined.

6 Bring the cream mixture back to a barely simmer over medium heat. Pour the warm cream mixture into the yolk mixture, whisking constantly, until it is well blended. Mix in the tangerine juice.

7 Pour the custard through a fine-network sifter into a perfect bowl. Set the vanilla bean aside (see note) after removing any remaining custard and seeds from the mixture. Dispose of the zing.

8 Empty the stressed custard into the pre-arranged ramekins. After placing the baking dish in the oven, carefully fill the baking pan halfway up the sides of the ramekins with very hot water and cover the pan with foil.

9 Heat for 35 to 45 minutes (20 to 30 minutes if utilizing a convection broiler), or until the focal point of the custard wiggles marginally when a ramekin is delicately shaken.

10 Exchange the baking dish to a wire rack, reveal, and let the pots de crème cool totally.

11 Eliminate the ramekins from the water shower and cover them with saran wrap. Refrigerate for up to two days or at least eight hours. Keep it cold.

Variations: I like to use other citrus fruits like grapefruit, Meyer lemon, and key lime in my pot de crème. Go ahead and substitute any of those here, amounting to 1 tablespoon of extra sugar to the recipe.

Maple flan makes 8 servings and Miami loves flan, so I'm always developing new recipes. This one is truly scrumptious — not excessively sweet thus smooth and velvety. It's ideal any season yet makes an incredible occasion dessert any place you end up residing.

3 cups room-temperature heavy cream 14 teaspoon kosher salt 1 split vanilla bean (see note) 2/3 cup sugar 1 cup maple syrup (preferably Grade B dark amber) 7 large egg yolks 1 In a medium saucepan, combine the salt and heavy cream. Add all of the vanilla bean's seeds to the saucepan along with the bean itself. Cook over medium intensity until simply stewing, around 4 minutes. Eliminate the container from the intensity, cover, and put away for no less than 30 minutes.

2 Position a broiler rack in the focal point of the stove, and pre-heat the broiler to 300°F (275°F if utilizing a convection broiler).

3 Place eight 6-ounce ramekins in a baking dish with sides that are 2 inches high.

4 Combine the sugar and three tablespoons of water in a small saucepan. Cook over low heat,

stirring frequently, until the sugar dissolves and the liquid is clear. Increment the intensity to medium high, and bubble, without mixing, for 3 to 5 minutes, or until the sugar starts to become brilliant brown on the edges. Delicately twirl the dish over the intensity to level out the variety and cook for 2 to 3 minutes longer, or until the sugar becomes a brilliant shade of golden. Pour the liquid evenly into the ramekins, swirling each one to cover the bottom completely, carefully and quickly.

5 Bring the maple syrup to a boil over medium heat in a large saucepan. Simmer for 8 to 10 minutes, or until it is reduced to 34 cup, at a medium-low heat. Watch out for the pot, and diminish the intensity assuming the syrup takes steps to bubble over.

6 Take the pan off the fire. The vanilla bean should be removed from the cream mixture and gradually added to the pan. Blend with a whisk.

7 Whisk the egg yolks in a medium bowl until well combined. Pour the warm maple mixture into the egg yolks, whisking constantly, until well blended.

8 Pour the custard through a fine-network sifter into a spotless bowl.

9 Pour the custard into the baking pans for the prepared ramekins. After placing the baking pan in the oven, carefully fill it halfway up the sides of the ramekins with very hot water.

10 Firmly cover the dish with foil and heat for 45 to 55 minutes (25 to 35 minutes if utilizing a convection broiler), or until the focal point of the custard wiggles somewhat when a ramekin is delicately shaken.

11 Cover the baking pan and let the flans cool completely on a wire rack.

12 Cover the ramekins with plastic wrap after removing them from the water bath. Refrigerate for up to two days or at least eight hours.

13 To serve, invert the custards onto small plates by running a thin knife around the edge.

key lime cheesecake flan

SERVES 6 Not a cheesecake, not exactly a key lime pie, and not a conventional flan — what's going on here? A great blend of all that Florida brings to the table. This flan is my favorite to serve with toasted Italian meringue and, if possible, tropical fruits like pineapple, lychees, or mango on top.

1 Position a rack in the center of the oven and preheat the oven to 300°F (275°F if using a convection oven) 12 cup fresh key lime juice (from 14 to 16 key limes) 14 cup sugar 4 ounces cream cheese, at room temperature 14 teaspoon kosher salt 34 cup evaporated milk, at room

temperature 34 cup sweetened condensed milk, at room temperature 2 extra-large eggs, at room temperature 3 extra-

2 Organize six 6-ounce ramekins in a baking dish that has 2-inch-high sides.

3 Combine 12 cups of the sugar and 3 tablespoons of water in a small saucepan. Cook over low heat, stirring frequently, until the sugar is dissolved and the liquid is clear. Increment the intensity to medium-high, and bubble, without mixing, for 3 to 5 minutes, or until the sugar starts to become brilliant brown on the edges. Tenderly whirl the dish over the intensity to level out the variety and cook for 1 to 2 minutes more, or until the sugar becomes golden. Pour the liquid evenly into the ramekins, swirling each one to cover the bottom completely, carefully and quickly.

4 Beat the cream cheese, the remaining 14 cups of sugar, and the salt with an electric mixer fitted with a paddle attachment for about 2 minutes, until the mixture is fluffy and smooth.

5 Add the dissipated milk and dense milk and scratch down the sides of the bowl. Blend on low speed until very much mixed.

6 Add the vanilla and the egg whites and mix on low speed until just combined. Mix in the key lime juice until well combined.

7 Pour the custard through a fine-network sifter into a perfect bowl.

8 Pour the strained custard into the baking pans for the prepared ramekins. After placing the baking pan in the oven, carefully fill it halfway up the sides of the ramekins with very hot water.

9 Cover the pan tightly with foil and bake for 35 to 45 minutes, or 20 to 30 minutes if using a convection oven, or until a ramekin shakes gently in the center of the custard.

10 Exchange the baking skillet to a wire rack, reveal, and let the flans cool totally.

11 Eliminate the ramekins from the water shower and cover them with saran wrap. Refrigerate for up to two days or at least eight hours.

12 To serve, scrape any liquid caramel from the ramekins onto the custards by running a thin knife around the edge and inverting them onto small plates.

Cinni mini bun pudding makes 8 servings It's safe to say that over the course of my career, I've made hundreds of bread puddings. It is an excellent method for completely transforming day-old, less-than-fantastic baked goods into something fantastic. Espresso cake pieces, corn biscuits, croissants, doughnuts, and even Twinkies taste perfect. Cinni Mini Bun Bites look too cute and taste amazing in bread pudding. However, this will not be possible if Cinni Minis are left over. For this recipe, make a batch of minis.

2 cups heavy cream, 12 cup sugar, 14 teaspoon kosher salt, 1 split vanilla bean (see note), 1 tablespoon finely grated tangerine zest, 4 large room-temperature egg yolks, 12 recipe (about 18) Cinni Mini Bun Bites, 4 ounces room-temperature cream cheese, cut into pieces 12 inches long Remove all of the vanilla bean's seeds and add them, along with the bean and the zest, to the saucepan. Cook for about 5 minutes over medium heat until just barely boiling.

2 Eliminate the skillet from the intensity and put away for 15 minutes.

3 Take the vanilla bean out, add any custard and seeds that are still in the mixture, and then set it aside (see note).

4 Whisk the egg yolks and the remaining 1/4 cup of sugar in a large bowl until well combined.

5 Bring the cream mixture back to a simmer over medium heat. Slowly pour it into the yolk mixture while continuously whisking until it is well blended. Throw in the Cinni Little Bun Nibbles and mix to cover.

6 Allow the bites to soak up the custard for 20 minutes, stirring occasionally, before serving. The nibbles ought to be delicate and stacked with custard prior to baking.

7 Position a rack in the focal point of the broiler, and preheat the stove to 350°F (325°F if utilizing a convection broiler). Place an 8-cup baking dish or eight 1-cup ramekins in a larger baking dish with 2-inch-high sides and lightly grease it, preferably with Pam.

8 Empty the custard combination into the more modest baking dish and uniformly disperse the cream cheddar pieces over the top. Put the baking dishes in the stove and fill the bigger baking dish with exceptionally high temp water to come mostly up the sides of the inward dish.

9 Bake for forty minutes, or approximately thirty minutes if using ramekins; 25 to 35 minutes (or until the pudding's top is lightly browned and the center jiggles slightly when lightly shaken if using a convection oven).

10 Remove the inner baking dish from the hot water bath and transfer the baking dishes to a wire rack. The bread pudding can be served right away or left to cool completely before being covered and stored in the refrigerator for up to three days.

Sweet corn and blueberry bread pudding is good for 9 to 12 people. Growing up in Philadelphia, New Jersey-grown Silver Queen corn and fresh blueberries were my favorite summertime flavors.

I still recall the buttery sweetness of the corn and the enormous blueberries' slightly tart snap and sweet finish. Combining flavors that aren't normally thought of together in a dessert is easy with this method.

I wish I could tell you a wonderful story about how this recipe came to be, but it didn't happen intentionally. I had some corn ice cream base left over that was too good to throw away and too little to churn. So I added blocks of brioche, new blueberries, and corn portions to it, making another most loved summer dessert.

6 ears corn

2 cups weighty cream

2 cups creamer

1 cup granulated sugar

½ teaspoon fit salt

2 vanilla beans, split (see note)

An additional 9 enormous egg yolks

8 cups 1½-inch blocks of challah or brioche, outside layers managed (day-old bread works best)

1 16 ounces new blueberries, washed and dried

2 tablespoons turbinado sugar

1 Shuck the corn and strip away the silk. Place the tip of an ear on a cutting board at an angle of 45 degrees while holding the stem end. Cut away the kernels with a sharp knife from the stem to the tip, rotating the ear until all of the kernels are removed. Continue with the other ears. You'll wind up with around 6 cups of pieces.

2 Add the cream, half-and-half, 2/3 cup of the sugar, and salt to the kernels and cobs in a large saucepan. Remove all of the vanilla beans' seeds from them and add them to the saucepan with the beans. Approximately 5 minutes, cook over medium-high heat until just barely boiling. Simmer for 20 minutes at a low temperature.

3 Set the pan aside for 15 minutes after removing it from the heat.

4 Utilizing utensils, eliminate the cobs from the custard, scratching any leftover fluid back into the blend, and throw them out. Remove the vanilla beans from the mixture and discard them, making sure to incorporate any remaining custard and seeds into the mixture (see note). Working in groups, strain the blend through a fine-network sifter set over a pan, solidly pushing on the portions with the rear of a spoon to separate each and every piece of flavor and cream. There will be about 4 cups of liquid left over; on the off chance

that it's not exactly that, add a touch all the more cream.

5 Whisk the egg yolks and the remaining 13 cups of sugar in a large bowl until well combined.

6 Bring the cream mixture back to a simmer over medium heat. Slowly pour it into the yolk mixture while continuously whisking until it is combined.

7 Add the bread and blueberries and mix to cover the bread. Put away for 20 minutes, blending incidentally, to permit the bread to ingest the custard.

8 Position a rack in the focal point of the broiler, and preheat the stove to 350°F (325°F if utilizing a convection stove). Place an 8-cup baking dish (I use an 8 x 8 x 2-inch pan) in a larger baking dish with 2-inch-high sides and lightly grease it, preferably with Pam.

9 Fill the smaller baking dish with the custard mixture. The larger baking dish should be filled halfway up the sides of the inner dish with extremely hot water after the baking dishes have been placed in the oven. The turbinado sugar should be evenly distributed on top. Bake for 43 to 45 minutes, or until the pudding's top is lightly browned and the center shakes a little when gently shaked.

10 Exchange both baking dishes to a wire rack. The bread pudding can be served right away or

cooled totally, covered, and refrigerated for as long as 3 days.

self-contradicting chocolate pudding

SERVES 8 TO 10 Puddings are so natural to make. I don't understand why, as a culture, we buy chocolate pudding that doesn't contain chocolate and comes pre-packaged with chemicals added to it. Each time I make this one, I'm floored by the smooth surface and the right in front of you chocolate wantonness. Pudding at home is very easy to make and well worth the effort. If desired, top with a spoonful of whipped cream.

An additional 6 huge egg yolks, at room temperature

⅔ cup sugar

2 tablespoons regular dim cocoa powder (ideally Valrhona)

1½ cups entire milk

1½ cups weighty cream

¼ teaspoon genuine salt

8 ounces ambivalent chocolate (ideally Valrhona Caraibe 66%), slashed

2 tablespoons (¼ stick) unsalted spread, cut into 3 pieces and at room temperature

2 teaspoons vanilla bean glue or unadulterated vanilla concentrate

1 In a medium bowl, whisk the egg yolks, sugar, and cocoa powder until mixed.

2 Heat the heavy cream, salt, and milk in a medium saucepan over medium heat until just

boiling. Slowly pour it into the yolk mixture while continuously whisking; then empty everything back into the pan.

3 Cook over medium-low intensity, mixing continually with a heatproof spatula — ensuring you get the sides and lower part of the pot — until the pudding is sufficiently thick to intensely cover the spatula and to hold a line drawn through it with your finger, around 3 to 5 minutes. The combination will enlist 170°F on a treats thermometer.

4 Add the chopped chocolate, butter, and vanilla after removing the pan from the heat. Stir until the chocolate and butter are smooth and melted.

5 Pour the pudding into a clean bowl that is one quart in size through a fine-mesh strainer. Refrigerate for at least 4 hours or up to 2 days by

pressing buttered parchment paper or plastic wrap directly onto the pudding's surface.

pumpkin streusel brioche bread pudding

SERVES 12 TO 16 When special times of year are coming and you're overreacting attempting to choose what to make for the parents in law (in the event that not the Maple Flan), search no farther than this recipe. Any member of the family who is picky and only wants pumpkin pie will be swayed by this bread pudding. It is a substantial recipe that is ideal for care package leftovers or late-night snacks. The Bacon Maple Pecan Ice Cream will make it a new family favorite when you serve it with it.

This recipe is dedicated to my dear friend Kay, who went on to become one of my most ardent supporters. She dreamed about this bread pudding all year because she was so in love with it. She and I were in love with it.

FOR THE STREUSEL

1¾ cups cake flour, filtered

½ cup granulated sugar

½ cup (stuffed) dull earthy colored sugar

½ cup cleaved pecans

1 teaspoon ground cinnamon (ideally Saigon, see note)

½ teaspoon legitimate salt

10 tablespoons (1¼ sticks) unsalted spread, softened and cooled

FOR THE PUDDING

2 cups weighty cream

2 cups cream

⅔ cup granulated sugar

3 tablespoons finely hacked new ginger

1 tablespoon finely ground tangerine zing

½ teaspoon ground cinnamon (ideally Saigon, see note)

½ teaspoon newly ground nutmeg

¼ teaspoon ground allspice

¼ teaspoon ground cloves

¼ teaspoon ground cardamom

¼ teaspoon legitimate salt

2 vanilla beans, split (see note)

An additional 9 huge egg yolks, at room temperature

1 (15-ounce) can pumpkin purée

2 tablespoons cognac or liquor

10 cups 1½-inch 3D shapes of challah or brioche, outside layers managed (day-old bread works best)

1 To make the fixing, in a medium bowl, consolidate the flour, sugars, pecans, cinnamon, and salt and mix until mixed. Stir in the cooled melted butter until well combined. The mixture should be very cold and the pieces should be about 34-inch clumps. Refrigerate for at least 20 minutes. Keep refrigerated until prepared to utilize.

2 Combine the heavy cream, half-and-half, sugar, ginger, tangerine zest, cinnamon, nutmeg, allspice, cloves, cardamom, and salt in a large saucepan to make the pudding. Remove all of the vanilla beans' seeds from them and add them to the saucepan with the beans. Approximately 5 minutes, cook over medium-high heat until the sugar is dissolved and just barely boiling.

3 Eliminate the container from the intensity, cover, and put away for no less than 30 minutes. Fish out the vanilla beans, scratching any leftover custard and seeds once again into the combination, and put them away (see note).

4 Whisk the cognac, pumpkin purée, and egg yolks in a large bowl.

5 Bring the cream mixture back to a simmer over medium heat. Slowly pour it into the yolk mixture while continuously whisking until well blended. Stir the bread in to coat.

6 Allow the bread to absorb the custard for 20 minutes by stirring occasionally.

7 Position a broiler rack in the focal point of the stove, and preheat the broiler to 350°F (325°F if utilizing a convection stove). Place a 12-cup baking dish lightly greased (preferably with Pam) in a larger baking pan with 2-inch-high sides (I use a 9 x 13-inch pan).

8 Empty the custard combination into the more modest baking dish. Put the baking dishes into the stove and cautiously fill the bigger baking dish with extremely boiling water to come mostly up the sides of the internal dish. Prepare for 20 minutes (15 minutes if utilizing a convection stove).

9 Eliminate the dish from the broiler and dissipate the streusel uniformly over the custard. Prepare for another 35 to 40 minutes (20 to 25 minutes if

utilizing a convection broiler), or until the fixing is brilliant brown and the focal point of the pudding wiggles marginally when the dish is delicately shaken.

10 Remove the inner baking dish from the hot water bath and transfer the baking dishes to a wire rack. The bread pudding can be served right away or left to cool completely before being covered and stored in the refrigerator for up to three days.

basil panna cotta makes six servings. Nothing else comes close to the fragrant experience that fresh herbs provide. Even though this recipe is great without the addition of any herbs, it is spectacular when made with basil, which I keep referring to as the new mint. This panna cotta is a favorite of Michael Schwartz, the chef and owner of Michael's Genuine Food & Drink. It demonstrates his belief in straightforward flavors. If you start with great ingredients and keep things simple, the end result will be fantastic.

1 vanilla bean, split (see note), 1 cup sugar, 1 cup packed fresh basil leaves, washed and dried, 1 tablespoon finely grated lemon zest, 1 pinch of kosher salt, 4 teaspoons unflavored powdered gelatin, 2 cups room-temperature buttermilk, 2 cups mixed fresh berries, washed and dried, for serving Strawberry consommé, 1 Pour the heavy cream into a medium saucepan. Add the vanilla bean, all of its seeds, sugar, basil, lemon zest, and salt to the saucepan along with the bean. Cook

over medium intensity until simply bubbling, around 5 minutes.

2 Cover the pan, set it aside for at least 30 minutes, and turn off the heat.

3 In a little bowl, sprinkle the gelatin north of 4 teaspoons of water and saved to mellow and sprout.

4 Remove the vanilla bean and set it aside, incorporating any custard and seeds that are still present into the mixture (see note).

5 Bring the cream mixture back to a simmer over medium heat.

6 Remove the pan from the heat and stir in the gelatin that has softened until it dissolves.

7 Pour the custard through a fine-network sifter into a perfect bowl, pushing on the basil and the zing to ensure you get all of the flavor from them. Dispose of the basil and the zing.

8 Add the buttermilk to the cream combination, and mix until very much mixed.

9 Empty the custard into 6 little straight-sided rocks glasses (around 6 ounces each, the thoughtful you would use for a decent whiskey). Refrigerate the glasses for at least eight hours or up to two days by covering them with plastic wrap.

10 To serve, spoon the berries on top of the panna cotta and pour a portion of the Strawberry Consommé over the organic product, whenever wanted. The consommé adds color and a delicious berry flavor.

Dishes Intercontinental

Accordingly, many flavors tracked down their direction into North African food. Newness and various flavors are fundamental in North African cooking.

In the souks, which are markets lined with open-fronted stalls typically found in the old neighborhoods of cities, people can purchase freshly ground herbs and spices. The sellers pile enormous mounds of spices on top of each other, creating a colorful rainbow and a delicious variety of scents. The business sectors likewise have a great deal of new spices, fish, grains, new and dried fava beans, lentils, and olive oil containers.

The souk is a feast for the senses and eyes.

Imagine a porridge with either millet, a type of grain, or chickpea flour and no coffee. Fresh fruit and flatbread are occasionally consumed. Egyptian morning meals incorporate tea and ful, otherwise called prepared beans.

In North Africa, the essential dinner of the day is al-ghada, or lunch. It usually starts with mezze, also called canapés. These reach from a basic choice of vegetable wedges, olives, or nuts to a gigantic collection of enticing cooked rarities. Perhaps a tagine, a substantial stew served in a similar stoneware pot and typically accompanied by a large platter of couscous, will arrive immediately. For dessert, either newly introduced regular items or prepared goods receive mint tea.

Al-acha, or dinner, may consist of just one meat or fish dish, a few appetizers, or a good soup.

In North Africa, hospitality is a highly prized tradition. Individuals take incredible consideration to show an extravagant cluster of dishes and guarantee that everybody is fulfilled when they set up a dinner for visitors.

Despite the growing popularity of Western-style tables and chairs, meals are typically served on large trays on low wooden stools with round bases. Plate made of copper, metal, or silver have perplexing examples cut into them. Pads encompass the plate, giving seating to people. Despite the rise in the use of forks and knives, many people still eat with their fingers. Correctly doing so is a delicate and refined art.

A young family member cleans the hands of the guests in a pretty basin filled with warm water at the beginning of the meal. Several drops of scented water are sprinkled on the dry hands.

Only the thumb and the first two fingers of the right hand are used when eating from the common dish on the plate.

Prayer is said before and after the meal. by muttering "Bismillah!" The host requests favor from Allah (God). Prior to the feast, in God's Name") Around the consummation of the dinner, visitors offer thanks by saying

Hamdullah ("Thanks be to God").

Even though each country in North Africa observes its own set of public holidays, they all celebrate the same Islamic religious holidays with loved ones. There is always a lot of food at the celebrations. Guests are welcomed with open arms and given free food and beverages. To decline is beyond comprehension.

Muslims observe a lunar calendar in which the new moon marks the beginning of each month. The Islamic lunar calendar is approximately 11 days shorter than the 365-day Western calendar. Since each Islamic month begins 11 days sooner than the beyond one, the dates of Muslim celebrations and events change over time one year to another.

The majority of Muslim holidays and celebrations center on significant occurrences in the life of Muhammad, the Arab prophet and founder of Islam. The Hegira recognizes Muhammad's getaway from Mecca, where individuals started to oppress him, and his appearance in Medina, both in what is presently Saudi Arabia. The two occasions happened in the year 622. Hegira marks the beginning of the Islamic new year. Meelad-ul-Nabal praises the Prophet's presentation. On the birthday of Fatimah, Muhammad's daughter, Women's Day is observed.

In the Tunisian city of Kairouan, the festival of Muhammad's birthday takes on additional importance. It is said that on the off chance that Muslims in Tunisia visit this city multiple times, they can satisfy their strict commitment to go on a journey. The joyful occasion, which is celebrated in Tunisia as Mouled or Moulid an-Nabi, attracts pilgrims from all over the world. The city is adorned with floor coverings and trees, and lavishly lit souks are open all day. What's more, Mouled is a period for eating. On the morning of Mouled, almost everyone eats assida, a sweet pudding, to get the party started. Another popular dessert is makroudh, which are small cakes filled with dates and soaked in honey.

Laylat-ul-Isra commemorates the night that the heavenly messenger Jibril (Gabriel) transported the prophet Muhammad to paradise. Muslims accept that Muhammad concluded that Muslims ought to supplicate or discuss salah five times each day while going with God through the seven sky.

The holy month of Ramadan is the most significant occasion for Muslims. Muslims observe Ramadan as a way to remember Allah's gift of the Quran to Muhammad. On this particular day, people are seen fasting and pleading with God. The majority of Muslims avoid food and drink from dawn to dusk. Before dawn, a light breakfast is consumed. During the day, devoted Muslims go to administrations and mosques—places of love—to supplicate. After nightfall, a subsequent feast, such as harira—a Moroccan soup made with sheep, vegetables, chickpeas, and grains—is served to loved ones.

The fast of Ramadan is broken on Eid al-Fitr. Typically, this celebration begins with special prayers at an Image Not Available mosque. On this day, everyone has the opportunity to celebrate and reflect on the previous month. People spruce up, frequently in spotless clothing. Children receive sweets and cash as gifts from various individuals. Special meals are shared with friends and family. Main dishes vary between families.

Another significant Muslim holiday is the Gala of Penance, or Eid al-Adha. This event occurs during the annual pilgrimage to Mecca in Saudi Arabia, also known as the hajj. Muslims should endeavor to make the outing no less than once in the course of their life assuming they are actually ready to. On Eid al-Adha, the excursion of the pil grims is remembered. It also praises a story from the Quran in which Abraham is tempted to sacrifice his child to Allah but is stopped and compensated for his faith.

Muslims normally cook a sheep and give the meat to companions, neighbors, and the less lucky to remember this legend. A stew, such as a chicken tagine, can be eaten by those who are unable to afford such an extravagant meal. Similar to Eid al-Fitr, this celebration typically lasts a few days and includes family gatherings, trips to mosques, and possibly presents and toys.

Moussems are local celebrations and festivals in North Africa. People may move, sing, eat, and supplicate together during celebrations of a nearby harvest, market, or sacred individual. For instance, Morocco hosts the Almond Blossom Festival in the second week of February. The appearance of the blossoms is cause for celebration because of their brief duration.

Imilchil Moussem, or the Celebration of Life Partners, is possibly one of the most captivating celebrations in Morocco. Imilchil is a tiny town in the Chart Book Mountains. Most young people in the area get married when the moussem arrives. In old times, love bird couples were honored by a heavenly man, and they lived joyfully ever subsequent to, as per legend. A large number of people from the mountains congregate under tents for three days to move and celebrate.

At the end of October, people in the Algerian oasis of Taghit celebrate the date harvest. An oasis is a fertile area in a desert. The cherry and tomato harvests are celebrated in other Algerian towns.

Independence Day and other national holidays are observed in every nation in the North African region. For instance, March 20 is Independence Day in Tunisia. On July 5, it takes place in Algeria. On June 11, Libyans observe Flight Day, which commemorates the 1970 departure of English soldiers from the country, which had been home to their military bases ever since The Subsequent Incredible Conflict (1939-45).

The people of North Africa celebrate numerous national, regional, religious, or patriotic holidays and festivals with delectable food. You can also check out these divine treats. Enjoy!

If you know what's in a dish, no matter how fancy or simple it is, cooking it will be easier and more enjoyable. Some of the fixings that are used in North African cuisine might be unfamiliar to you. Despite the fact that any container and utensils can be utilized to make the recipes in this book, extraordinary cookware is at times utilized.

The main thing to realize prior to starting is the means by which to painstakingly cook. On the accompanying page, you'll discover a few hints that will make your cooking experience protected, fun, and simple.

The following segment is a "word reference" of terms, interesting cooking instruments, and fixings. You could likewise need to peruse the counsel on the best way to make solid, low-fat suppers.

Scrutinize the recipe completely at whatever point you've picked one to endeavor. You are now prepared to go shopping for the necessary cookware and ingredients. You can begin cooking once everything is assembled.

When you're cooking, there are a few safety precautions you should always follow. Even the best cooks adhere to these guidelines in the kitchen.

• Before handling food, always thoroughly wash your hands. Wash every natural and crude vegetable thoroughly to eliminate soil, synthetics, and insecticides. In ice water, clean raw meat, fish, and poultry.

- Utilize a cutting board while slashing vegetables and organic products.

You shouldn't be holding them cut up! Cut away from yourself and your fingers at the same time.

- If you wear loose clothing or have long hair, it's easy for them to catch fire. Tie your long hair back before you start cooking if you have it.

- To keep your sleeve or jewelry from getting caught on the pot handles, turn them all the way toward the stove's back. When members of the family are still young, this is especially crucial. They could certainly harm a pot by knocking it over.

- While disposing of compartment from the oven or standing hot pots, reliably use a pot holder. When cleaning a hot dish, try not to use a damp cloth because the steam that comes out of it could kill you.

- To avoid burning yourself, lift the lid of a steaming pot away from you.

- Assuming that you get singed, absorb the impacted region cold water.

Apply no oil or spread to it. Butter or grease only retains heat, whereas cold water aids in its removal.

- Throw baking soda or salt at the lower part of the fire to put it out if oil or cooking oil shoots into flares. An oil fire won't be extinguished by water.)

Try to turn all of the stove's burners to "off" while calling for assistance.

The health benefits of a Mediterranean diet, which is high in vegetables and natural foods, whole grains, nuts, and vegetables, have been recognized by food experts for a very long time. The majority of the protein that North Africans and other Mediterranean people consume comes from fish, chicken, and beans rather than red meat. Meat is not the main course; rather, it enhances the flavor of the basic course's vegetables and grains.

Many dishes already have low fat content because vegetables and legumes are used in so much of North African cooking. When sautéing, olive oil is typically used instead of spread, which typically reduces the amount of fat absorbed by the meal. You can occasionally reduce the total amount of oil used in a recipe, thereby further reducing fat.

In contrast to a lot of European and North American dishes, many North African recipes use a lot of spices and flavors to make their sauces taste and smell great. Cardamom, caraway, coriander, cumin, saffron, turmeric,

new cilantro, and mint leaves, got along with new vegetables,

lentils, dried beans, or couscous, can make a superb and fulfilling

dish. In many recipes that normally call for meat, you can use fish or poultry instead of sheep, or you can keep the dish vegetarian.

Instead of chocolate, butter, heavy cream, and sugar, many desserts from North Africa use honey, dates, raisins, almonds, filo dough, and other ingredients. Low-fat milk or cream can be substituted for richer, higher-fat ingredients in recipes, and margarine can be substituted for butter. However, these substitutes may alter the flavor and consistency of the dish in treats. Wedges of fresh natural product are always included in treats that are quick, healthy, and energizing.

The majority of dishes from North Africa are delicious and filling. Try out a variety of recipes and substitutions as you get better at cooking to find the ones that work best for you.

Regularly, food and drink are served on an enormous plate set on four low wooden legs or on a texture cover. On the floor or on low pads, the primary visitor is close to the host. Scooping is traditionally done with the right hand's fingers or flatbread pieces. In some countries, plates and cutlery are now more common.

The best treat of all is sampling the various dishes, regardless of whether your table is set with rich or plain plates.

Mezze consumption is a way of life in North Africa. Starters can be served toward the start of a dining experience or as a solitary nibble. There are more mezze options available for events that are more significant.

Goodies can be as transparent as various nuts, olives, tomato slices, or cucumber wedges. Then again, they could incorporate various plates of mixed greens and different dishes, both crude and cooked.

Hummus, a thick paste made of ground chickpeas, spices, and ground sesame seeds, is one of the most well-known North African appetizers for diners in North America. Pita bread, a flatbread that is popular in North Africa and the Middle East and can be purchased at specialty markets and supermarkets, is typically served with it.

This part presents only a couple of the numerous mezze dishes that North Africa brings to the table. Mezze are simply limited by your creative mind and the trimmings you have nearby.

Soups are commonly served around early afternoon, yet they can likewise be served at supper with mezze platters. Soups are frequently served as the first course after a day of fasting during Ramadan.

Any dinner in North Africa can be paired with leafy greens. A wide range of fruits, legumes, and vegetables are used to make them. Dressings oftentimes contain cayenne pepper, salt, lemon juice, and olive oil. The trimming could include olives or new spices like mint, cilantro, or parsley. For a salad, always select crisp, fresh vegetables.

Meat, fish, or poultry, as well as vegetables, vegetables, and grains, are typical trimmings in North African essential dishes. The most well-known meat in North Africa is sheep. In fact, lamb or mutton is frequently referred to as "meat" in the majority of contexts. Sheep, in contrast to cows, can move around effectively and can live in appalling fields. Another popular dish is chicken. Fish is a common dish for people who live near the Mediterranean Sea, but it is rare and expensive inland. Pork is against Muslim dietary law, and North African beef is unavailable.

Many North Africans use meat sparingly, almost as a seasoning. In any case, during special times of year, families might broil an entire sheep or sheep.

The stew known as the tagine is one of the region's most flavorful main dishes. In tagines, a particular blend of flavors and spices can be used alongside sheep, chicken, or fish in any way. They are typically cooked in a tagine, a traditional clay pot with a cover that is shaped like a cone. Regardless of the pot you use to slow cook your tagine, it still tastes good and is delicious.

Couscous, which many people consider to be the foundation of North African cuisine, is typically served with a tagine. Many households consume couscous several times per week, which is made of rolled semolina wheat in very small grains or pellets. The stew is typically placed in the middle of a hollow on a platter when it is served. It is both a culinary and visual treat.

People in North Africa frequently consume new organic products for dessert rather than heavy cakes and pies. In the middle of the year, new melon, grapes, and fragrant oranges might be served on platters. Winter treats include dates, dried apricots, raisins, and figs. Another well-known dessert is pudding, or custard, which is typically made with rice or semolina. These dishes are delicious and minimalist in design.

A variety of pastries made of thin dough, filled with nuts, and coated in sweet syrup are served on holidays and other special occasions. Even though lighter desserts are common, wealthy households may serve this kind of pastry more often. The sweets are accompanied by a minty sweet tea. It's impolite of dinner guests to turn down dessert, no matter how full they are.

Event meals are get-togethers went to by friends and family in North Africa. Numerous festival tables are loaded with olives, new organic product, newly heated flatbread, and extraordinary recipes for sheep, chicken, and fish. Khtayef, which are nuts, honey, and sugar-based thin dough-based sweet pastries, round out the meal. They are accompanied by sweet mint tea or thick coffee.

The majority of Middle Easterners consider meat to be an unnecessary luxury, and virtually no meat is used in typical cooking. Regardless, events are an exception. On those days, people might get together with friends and family to share a whole roast lamb or sheep.

Good food is enjoyable to savor.

Eating is clearly fundamental for perseverance, yet it is likewise one of life's inconceivable joys. We make our dining experiences social since we appreciate eating to such an extent. We accumulate with our families and companions around tables loaded up with nutritious food.

However, our pleasure has also evolved into a risk. Today, our relationship with food — or, to be more exact, our voracious hunger for explicit food varieties — is regularly destructive to our wellbeing. I'm looking at rising obesity rates as a result of our unhealthy eating habits, which are linked to diabetes, heart disease, stroke, and other diseases. Accepting you've been examining news magazines and periodicals lately, you comprehend what I mean.

Experts taught us for a long time that the only way to remain muscular and lean was to give up many of our favorite foods and make sacrifices to keep a healthy weight. Many of us began the difficult road to health, but we did not always arrive. Clearly unsuitable for long-term weight management, many well-known diets are designed for short-term weight loss. The South Beach Diet, on the other hand, was designed to prevent heart attacks and strokes by reducing waistlines and enhancing blood chemistry. This implies carrying on with a sound way of life as opposed to only searching for a handy solution.

Identifying the Main Cause of the Problem: What precisely is the problem? Most of the time, new research has shed light on previously obscure aspects of our bodies' processes for handling food. The significant effects of fiber, glycemic index (the rate at which a food raises glucose), good fats, and pre-diabetes on health and weight were only recently recognized.

Consumes less calories, then again, additionally fizzled on the grounds that they didn't consider how regular individuals capability. Most of the diets used to lose weight were strict, time-consuming, and unnatural. They requested that we surrender totally the joys of eating a wide assortment of delicious food sources in adequate amounts to fulfill our craving and joy our palates until the end of our lives.

I saw firsthand how the false information we were fed about diets and weight loss led us astray. My primary focus as a cardiologist has been the balance of coronary disease. My proudest accomplishment to date is my dedication to the development of a heart filter convention that makes use of electron pillar mechanized tomography (EBT) technology. This technology is able to quickly and easily identify the development of arteriosclerosis in the walls of corridors years before it causes respiratory failure or stroke. From one side of the world to the other, the degree of coronary calcium (or plaque, as you could know it) is proposed as the Agatston Score.

By identifying issues that would not have been detected otherwise and treating them prior to requiring surgery, this technology has saved many lives. This test may not prevent heart disease on its own, despite its ability to detect issues early. However, some medications and lifestyle adjustments, such as regularly exercising and eating a healthy diet, can help prevent heart attacks. I was stuck in this realm. As other cardiologists, I advised my patients to adhere to the low-fat diet recommended by the American Heart Association and other specialists to reduce weight and cholesterol levels. However, things didn't go as planned. The low-fat program was followed by a few patients, but they did not lose much weight. If they followed the diet and exercise plan, a few would lose weight and feel fine. Nevertheless, at some point, they might become exhausted as a result of their incessant hunger, neglect their primary sources of nutrition, or simply lose control. They'd start bamboozling sometimes by then, at that point, and in what might seem like no time, all the extra weight was back on. They frequently gained more weight than before they went on a diet. Crash diets actually slow down our metabolism, making us more likely to yo-yo diet. Truth be told, various examinations have recorded the disappointments of speedy weight reduction systems and low-fat, high-carb counts calories.

The low-fat diet became the standard for weight loss across the country despite the lack of scientific evidence for its effectiveness. We were told how awful cheddar, meat, eggs, and even oil from a plate of mixed greens are. As a direct consequence of this, manufacturers of foodstuffs began developing a brand-new category of products that they referred to as "low-fat" or "low-cholesterol." This category included everything from hot dogs to cookies to potato chips to salad dressing. Similarly, the food selections were lower in cholesterol or fat. There was only one issue: The "handled" carbs—mostly white sugar itself, high fructose corn syrup, honey, molasses, and starches—had replaced the fats and cholesterol. They also did not contain any fiber or supplements.

Individuals were allowed to relish these food varieties thus. Sadly, I was one of the low-fat eaters; what a mistake! We weren't aware that we were ingesting more sugars and starches than ever before. Our blood sugar levels were changing quickly and significantly as a result, making us hungry again shortly after eating a meal or snack. The outcome was the public scourge of heftiness and diabetes, which is presently broad around the world.

The "Good Fats" I began my own research into the nutrition and weight loss literature after becoming dissatisfied with the low-fat, high-carb approach and witnessing some success with other high-saturated-fat, low-carb diets. I needed to find a smart diet plan that would not only help my patients eat well but also help them get in shape and have better blood tests.

The flaws in the plan for eating low-fat foods became immediately apparent. The so-called saturated fats, which are primarily found in animal products like butter, cheese, fatty meats, and cream, did in some way contribute to obesity. Nonetheless, fundamentally short of what we had been persuaded to think. Their essential wellbeing risk was that they added to raised cholesterol and unsaturated fats, which prompted cardiovascular illness. As a cardiologist, I was worried about that.

However, there are also solid fats, particularly Mediterranean oils like extra-virgin olive oil, canola oil, omega-3 fish oils, and the majority of nuts' oils. They are not a danger. They are not level headed. We think they're fantastic. They help break down sugar and insulin, making it easier to keep a healthy weight and lowering the risk of heart attacks and strokes over time.

I discovered during my research that carbohydrates and fats cannot be grouped in the same way. There are good and bad carbs, just like there are good and bad fats. More specifically, there is a wide assortment of starches, going from very unwanted to genuinely satisfactory to incredibly attractive. A well-balanced diet relies heavily on healthy carbs.

Starches like beans, organic products, and vegetables have never been addressed for their advantages. On the other hand, back when the anti-fat gospel was still prevalent, we were taught that even the most starchy, refined carbohydrates like white bread, white pasta, potatoes, and instant rice were healthy. Nonetheless, our endeavors to get more fit were really prevented by these food sources.

All starches, including the best vegetables, contain sugars. Rice, potatoes, and wheat flour are all examples of starches, which are nothing more than sugar molecule chains. Our bodies get rid of those sugars during digestion and put them to good use, giving us the energy we need. We would perish without sugar.

Notwithstanding, before we can get to these starches, our stomach related frameworks should isolate the sugars from the fiber. Grateful for that, that fiber dials back the cycle that influences the stomach. It suggests that the sugars enter our bloodstream gradually. At the point when that occurs, the sign is gotten by the pancreas, what starts creating insulin. Insulin is answerable for shipping this glucose into our cells, where it very well may be utilized right away or put away for sometime in the future.

However, when we consume carbohydrates with very little or no fiber at all, something very different happens. At the point when that happens, our stomach related frameworks start quickly handling the sugars in general. The pancreas releases a lot of insulin at once as a result of the sharp rise in blood sugar, or glucose. In point of fact, the pancreas might react too strongly and make more insulin than is needed. As a result, the level of glucose drops dramatically.

Even though you don't know everything that's going on in your body, you can actually feel it through a sense that's more indirect. Hunger is stoked by the thrilling rise and fall of glucose. Your metabolism simply causes changes in the chemistry of your blood, which in turn causes hunger. You become more insatiable on account of this particular sensation sooner than you would normally. In addition, the craving is for more carbohydrates.

The inclination of a food to modify glucose levels is estimated by the glycemic record, or GI. David Jenkins, M.D., Ph.D., of the University of Toronto, developed it in the 1980s. This basic idea was inaccessible to the makers of prior abstains from food. The GI framework ranks food sources based on how quickly they raise glucose in comparison to 50 grams of glucose, which has a GI of 100. Food X will only raise glucose half as quickly as glucose if it has a GI of half. Dr. Jenkins' glycemic index demonstrated to us that white potatoes raise blood sugar more rapidly than table sugar. What significance does this have? After a meal, your blood sugar rises and falls more quickly. In point of fact, if you consume something with a high glycemic index, your blood sugar is more likely to rise quickly and then return to where it was prior to the meal. Emotions such as irresistible cravings, severe fatigue, sleepiness, headaches, and anxiety are all brought on by this blood sugar roller coaster.

At the point when receptive hypoglycemia happens, the primary carbs that raise glucose are normally consumed. You look for foods that quickly lower your symptoms and quickly raise your glucose levels. This starts a loop that never ends. Your body takes some time to realize that its blood sugar levels have returned to normal, so you continue to eat during this time because you are not yet full. As a result, you consume a lot of food without realizing it, which intensifies glucose fluctuations and restarts the cycle. This example is responsible for the nationwide epidemic of diabetes and obesity.

These realities have forever been the groundwork of human digestion. Be that as it may, the market's accentuation on fast, straightforward, and advantageous cooking clashes with the manner in which our bodies cycle food. For instance, everything that is made with white flour has had virtually all of the fiber removed from it. This incorporates every prepared great, including most of breads, wafers, and biscuits delivered in a business setting. The same is true for breakfast cereals like instant oatmeal that claim to be healthy. Doughnuts, cakes, cookies, and other sweet treats are also included in this category. waffles and pancakes, as well. Indeed, even rice has been processed to facilitate cooking; the fiber has been removed, allowing for quicker preparation.

When you cut out fiber, you also cut out a lot of vitamins and minerals that fiber contains. These carbs have been referred to as "void calories" in this way. They give us only calories and nothing else our bodies need to function properly. Additionally, the fiber slows down the absorption of carbohydrates. It aids in the gradual and consistent storage of sugar (energy) by our bodies, allowing us to function effectively for extended periods of time without experiencing hypoglycemia symptoms.

Reversing the Trend In what ways can the obesity crisis be stopped? Healthy, solid fats, regular nutrients and supplements, and a diet high in healthy carbs are our new norm. To put it another way, we follow the South Sea side Eating schedule.

As I stated, bad carbs can be found in a variety of places. They include all of the snacks that have become so prevalent in modern eating, making them the most convenient foods. Some people are drawn to salty snacks like pretzels and potato chips, which are high in bad carbs. Others indulge in baked goods, ice cream, or chocolate due to a persistent sweet tooth. Cravings for rice, potatoes, bread, or pasta plague some people. No matter what the goal is, the finished product is the same: When we consume a lot of highly processed carbohydrates, our bodies become overloaded and experience an increased craving. It is a strange peculiarity that the food we consume actually increases our appetite rather than satisfying it.

Some diet experts joined the anti-carbohydrate camp when this physiology became clear. All carbs were suddenly recognized as the primary contributor to obesity. In point of fact, a diet that is too low in sugar will not include enough supplements, regular nutrients, or dietary fiber, all of which are necessary for maintaining optimal health.

Besides, individuals appreciate eating sugars. It radiated an impression of being a horrible stumble to give up food sources like bread, pasta, rice, and, shockingly, a couple of results of the dirt. Also, by this time, we had all gone through enough weight loss programs where we had to give up foods we liked. It is conceivable to eat carbs, even bread and rice, etc, as long as the grains have not been irrationally managed. People who are trying to lose weight can consume carbohydrates if the whole grain is still present.

If you eat the right fats, like olive oil, nuts, avocados, and omega-3 fish oils, you can still lose weight and improve your health. Additionally, the presence of healthy fats enhances the flavor of our food. This is one more motivation behind why they are so urgent toward the South Ocean side Eating regimen.

The South Pacific side's diet: Finding some kind of equilibrium At this point, I realized that a diet that was healthy would not be low in carbohydrates or fat. Our weight issue had been invited on instead of fixed by those cutoff points. A healthy diet and exercise plan would differentiate between good and bad carbohydrates and fats. Dieters would be able to eat enough healthy foods so that they wouldn't really miss the bad ones.

That was the South Beach Diet's central concept.

A lot of foods that taste good and fill you up would be used on the diet: Using flavorful sauces and spices, healthy fats like extra virgin olive oil are used to cook meat, poultry, seafood, and vegetables.

Another requirement was that the food be served in portions large enough to satisfy a typical appetite. It is impossible for anyone to go hungry all the time. The South Beach Diet recommends spreading out your snacking throughout the day as a result.

I know what a pastry is because I love chocolate. In any case, sweets are allowed during the strictest stage because the South Oceanside Eating Plan is designed to allow you to eat as normally as possible. I think that this book has some great recipes for desserts that not only taste great but can also be enjoyed without making you gain weight. In many of the dessert recipes, fruit and a sugar substitute that doesn't have any calories are used. Instead of saturated or trans fats, which can be bad for your health, choose healthy fats whenever possible.

Those who have read The South Pacific Diet are aware that there are three stages to the program. The first stage typically takes a very long time and is usually prohibitive. All starches, including breads, rice, pasta, and arranged foods, are destroyed by it. Additionally, it restricts all sugars, including alcohol and those found in fruits. The second phase continues until you reach your goal weight. You add liquor, natural sugars with low glycemic index, and starches like whole grains to dinners. At the point when you arrive at your objective weight, you enter the upkeep stage, the third stage. The eating routine has evolved into a way of life—a better way to eat that lets you eat what you need while maintaining your health and getting in shape at the same time. If you choose a sweet potato over a white one, brown rice over white, and whole grain bread over white, you still remember what you learned in the first two phases. You have figured out the order of the various classes of starches and how to use them in your daily life after taking everything into account.

If a lot of the South Beach Diet's recipes and meals are delicious and simple to prepare, it's more than just a diet plan. There are more than 200 options in this cookbook to keep your meals interesting and new.

All the best for your happiness and success!

You'll need to change how you shop if you change how you eat. Truth be told, it will change how you cook, which will decide if health food nuts succeed. I meant to say that it is where you win or lose, but you actually win this challenge!!) Notwithstanding, when you start the South Ocean side Eating regimen, your storage space, cooler, and fridge ought to all look altogether different — and, obviously, much better.

It is difficult to exaggerate that it is so significant to eat the right food sources and stay away from some unacceptable food varieties. When I talk to people who have stopped following the diet, I continue to hear the same important story: I got back subsequent to working all day late, I was starving, and there were no vegetables in the fridge — so I microwaved a sack of frozen french fries considering everything." " On the other hand, there was no sugar gelatin dessert, so I had a cupcake. As an illustration, "I ate a few pretzels, washed down with a pop," as I ran out of almonds. You can eat a wide range of delicious foods on the South Beach Diet. You will not need to monitor how much or the number of calories you that consume. However, avoiding truly unhealthy products that will hinder your success is absolutely necessary.

Regardless of how enthusiastically you try, it won't always be difficult. Something as simple as a loaf of bread can become a source of contention when one partner is on a diet and the other is not; The dieter may wish for it to go away while the partner still uses it for their daily sandwich. One member of a family I know has stopped buying bread altogether, and the husband now only buys one new roll for dinner each night. When you're a health food nut with kids, it can be especially difficult because you can't stop the kids from getting their little treats, but it might be hard to stop yourself from attacking the treat compartment. Naturally, willpower is required, but if you can convince the kids to enjoy fudge pops without added sugar, everyone will benefit.

It's critical to keep your kitchen South Ocean side Eating routine well disposed if you have any desire to eat better and get in shape. Before you start the diet, this chapter will show you what groceries you need to buy. The list includes foods that are allowed in Phase 1—the initial, strict phase—as well as in Phases 2 and 3, which are less restrictive stages. Phase 1 is the strict phase. I want to assist you in designing a kitchen that is balanced, healthy, and well-appointed so that you can eat well and lose weight in the coming weeks or months.

None of the things on this list are required of you to purchase them; Allow your instincts to guide you. Simply having enough of your favorite foods on hand should be your objective. You won't even need or have room for anything else if you eat well. Everything you'd find in a well-stocked supermarket should be included in this. On the off chance that you can't find a thing where you shop, you can skip it and get another.

Cleaning the Storeroom But before you go shopping, you might have to clear some space in your kitchen. As a result, the first step is to get rid of any foodstuffs that don't adhere to the South Pacific Diet. This includes your refrigerator, freezer, and other storage areas. For the first two weeks of the diet, some foods can be stored; They will be permitted once more after that. Various extravagances, particularly the most bothersome ones, ought to undoubtedly vanish forever. I swear, you won't remember them after the main meal.

An extensive parcel of the food assortments you can't eat during Stage 1 of the South Sea side Eating routine are on the going with overview, like specific food sources you can't eat during Stage 2. Even though the list is quite extensive, it would be difficult to include every food that calorie counters should avoid. Good advice is to adhere to the following: If it is one of the first three fixings, any structure with sugar, including fructose, maltose, dextrose, or anything else with sugar, is probably against the rules. During Stage 1, you can't make anything with flour. After that, you can't make anything with enriched white flour. However, whole wheat flour is healthier, and heated foods that do not contain at least 3 grams of fiber per serving should not be consumed.

As a result, before starting the first phase of the diet, clear out your kitchen of the following items:

Products baked: All waffles, cakes, waffles, treats, cupcakes, and saltines are remembered for this. In fact, even the finest whole wheat breads ought to disappear during Stage 1. English- and non-English-language muffins.

Beverages: Juices of any kind are not allowed for the first fourteen days of the agreement. Beverages containing sugar, fructose, corn syrup, and all sodas are prohibited.

Additionally, for Stage 1, no mixed drinks are available. This includes whiskey, beer, wine, wine coolers, and pre-mixed cocktails.

Cereals: For the first two weeks, all cereal varieties are off the diet. This includes solid grains like kashi and oats, which are high in fiber and low in sugar. The carbohydrates in a lot of business cereals cause a dangerous rise in glucose, which makes people want more carbs. Fiber-rich cereals are back in Stage 2.

Dressings, toppings, and flavors: It against the law against the law to use barbecue sauce, honey mustard, ketchup, or another fixing or sauce made with sugar, molasses, or corn syrup. Truth be told, barbecue sauces, mayonnaise, salad dressings, and other low-fat or without fat fixings can't be modified. Surprised? These items typically contain refined sugars in place of fat.

Due to its sugar content, the majority of commercial teriyaki sauce is also prohibited. Sweet pickles and relish are also denied.

Avoid all commercial salad dressings that are fat-free and contain sugar (including fructose) or carbohydrates. Vinegar and extra-virgin olive oil dressings are acceptable. Dressings that don't have sugar or carbs are also sufficient.

Dairy: Because it contains a lot of saturated fat, whole milk is against the South Beach Diet. Part-skim, sans fat, and different cheeses made with milk other than 2% are additionally restricted in Stage 1. Absolutely no brie or other creamy cheeses. Butter is extremely scarce.

Fish and shellfish: There are no fish to be killed. Safe are all fish, whether fresh or canned. The sleek fish like anchovies, mackerel, salmon, and sardines are particularly recommended because of the healthy omega-3 oils they contain.

Flour: Everything made of flour is illegal during Stage 1. Mix for pancakes or waffles is the same. Additionally, cornmeal is not permitted.

Fruit: During Stage 1, all of that natural substance is prohibited. Before fruits can be included in your diet again, you must eliminate them for two weeks. They not only have a lot of sugar in them, but they also make you hungry. The same category encompasses all fruit products, including jellies, jams, and dried fruits like raisins. During Phase 1, no fruit-containing frozen foods or fruit juice are permitted.

Poultry and meat: On the South Ocean side Eating routine, meat and poultry are abundant, yet some are denied. Honey-ready or maple-assuage ham, for instance, are both prohibited during all stages. The majority of the meats served at a lunch gathering are permitted; however, when purchasing packaged items, pay close attention to the fixings. Put it in a difficult spot expecting you see as any kind of sugar there.

During Stage 1, greasy birds like duck and goose ought not be served. Pâté is likewise illegal. Additionally, dark-meat turkey and chicken (legs and wings) are prohibited due to their higher cholesterol and fat content. Handling poultry, like bundled chicken strips or patties, is precluded at any stage. Breakfast hotdogs and bacon are high in saturated fat, so avoid them at all costs.

Dispose of any greasy rib, liver, or hamburger brisket steaks. Veal bosom is the same way.

Fats and oils: As you clear out your kitchen, dispose of solid areas for any shortening or oil.

Pasta: Pasta of any kind, including whole wheat, is not allowed for Stage 1.

Rice: Any sort of earthy colored rice is not feasible for the initial fourteen days.

Snacks: Snacks packaged in a salty or sweet form—like cheese puffs, popcorn, potato chips, pretzels, taco chips, and so on—as well as in both forms are prohibited.

In the event that we could take out undeniably handled food varieties from our eating regimen, our weight would drop and our general wellbeing would move along. It is difficult to lose weight with processed carbohydrates because they lack vitamins, minerals, and fiber.

The sort of carbs in these pungent or sweet bites decisively raise glucose, which makes you need more carbs. Because of the makers' endeavors to restore a portion of the supplements that have been lost, dealt with carbs are much of the time alluded to as "maintained" or "supplement upgraded." However, the health benefits of natural vitamins outweigh those of synthetic vitamins. Trans fats are also present in a lot of snack foods that are prepared commercially.

Soup: Avoid using powdered soup blends in your kitchen for the first 14 days because many of them contain trans fats. You can consume clear stock or reduced-fat canned bean soup at any time.

Sweeteners: Except for sugar substitutes, no sugars are permitted in Stage 1. Molasses, honey, brown sugar, white sugar, and corn syrup are all included in this.

Vegetables: Sincerely, even a few vegetables are required for Stage 1. Even if they are bubbled, potatoes are the best. The sugars are immediately isolated by your stomach related system, achieving set aside weight. Potatoes also encourage individuals to consume more bad carbs. White potatoes, sweet potatoes, and yams are all included in this.

Corn is also distant until extra warning, nearby beets, butternut squash, and oak seed squash. They are all immediately transformed into sugar, which makes you hungry. For the first two weeks, you should only consume carrots. Get rid of any frozen packaged foods that contain these vegetables by going through your freezer.

The Shopping Rundown for the South Pacific Diet
These are the foods that you should eat. This list is divided into two sections. The foods that can be eaten during Phase 1, the two weeks of the diet that are the most restrictive, are discussed in the first section. The second contains a list of what to eat during Phase 2.

For Stage 3, a rundown is unnecessary. You'll eat this way for the rest of your life, and you'll know enough about the plan to find the best options.

Purchasing heated products in Stage 1: Avoid any hot places for the entire fourteen days of Stage 1.

Beverages: Juiced espresso is allowed on a regular basis, but you shouldn't drink more than two cups a day because caffeine makes insulin. Unrestricted decaf is permitted. The same restrictions apply to tea consumption.

Evidently, water is safe. As long as the flavored water does not contain any calories, it is acceptable. Look hard and long at the names, beyond a shadow of a doubt. Seltzer and club soda are acceptable. If you prefer the flavored varieties, check to see that none of the ingredients contain any sugar.

Diet pop, chilled teas low in calories, and powdered drinks are OK. Powdered orange beverages with low calories, as light Gem's, are a famous breakfast refreshment for health food nuts. V8 juice or a similar vegetable mixed drink juice can be consumed.

Cereals: Cereals are not allowed in Stage 1.

Flavors, dressings, and garnishes: Make sure you have a lot of flavors that don't contain sugar. Almond and vanilla extracts on their own are also delicious. Any pepper assortment will do: dark, red, cayenne, and white are all acceptable flavors and preparations on this diet. In fact, I encourage you to use anything that makes food taste better. If your healthy options taste good, you won't be as tempted to eat unhealthy options. Try a few of the many seasonings and spices available at your neighborhood grocery store.

Spice things up with spices like curry, red pepper, or cumin, or try herbs like basil, oregano, and parsley. Garlic can be used in a variety of ways because it can be fresh, minced, or powdered. Nutmeg, cinnamon (ground, not cinnamon-sugar!), cloves will give a dish a cozy, warm flavor, while dill, rosemary, and mint will give it a strikingly fresh flavor. Seasonings, whether used individually or in combination, will give any dish new life.

Phase 1 cannot contain honey mustard, regular fat-free mayonnaise, chimichurri steak sauce, hot sauce or Tabasco, salsa, prepared horseradish, or light (low-sodium) soy sauce or Worcestershire sauce. Some delicious homemade condiments can be made using the recipes at the top of this page.

For dressing your servings of mixed greens, you can utilize any of the supported oils — canola, flaxseed, additional virgin olive oil, nut, sesame, or pecan — and vinegar — like balsamic or wine. Cardini's Original Caesar Salad Dressing, Newman's Own Light Balsamic Vinaigrette, and Newman's Own Olive Oil and Vinegar dressing are all acceptable among the prepared dressings. To be honest, any dressing that does not contain carbohydrates or sugar will suffice.

Dairy: Stay away from milk, yogurt, and all full-fat frozen yogurt during Stage 1. You can eat fat-free cottage cheese, fat-free plain yogurt, and milk with less than one percent fat up to twice a day. Dairy can also be substituted for plain low-fat soy milk. You are free to choose any reduced-fat cheddar you like. A good rule of thumb is to stick with cheeses that have about 6 grams of fat per serving. Part-skim ricotta, part-skim mozzarella, and curds made with either 1% or 2% milk fat are satisfactory cuts of American cheddar. Feta cheddar with less fat is a fair decision. However, if you are unable to locate reduced-fat feta, the standard variety is acceptable due to its delicious flavor and minimal preparation requirements.

Eggs: Even in Stage 1, you can eat eggs if your cholesterol has been raised in an unsafe way. If your doctor has advised you not to eat eggs, inquire about using an egg substitute. In sign of the real world, eggs aren't almost essentially as horrible as we normally thought they would be. They are an incredible regular wellspring of vitamin E and raise the degree of good cholesterol similarly to that of terrible cholesterol. Fish and shellfish: Halibut, herring, salmon, rainbow or lake trout, fish, and mackerel are among the allowed new fish. Sardines, whether fresh or canned, lox, canned salmon, canned fish, and smoked whitefish are all acceptable options. The eating routine consolidates mollusks, crab, lobster, shrimp, and various types of shellfish. Like meat, fish should be ready in a solid way. It should not to be seared or even breaded. There are numerous ways to prepare fish, including steamed, baked, grilled, sautéed, and roasted. Despite its high cholesterol content, a spot or two every now and then is acceptable.

Flour: During Phase 1, avoid using any flour.

Fruit: During Stage 1, avoid all unendingly regular item squeezes.

Poultry and meat: Most of meats are alright. They are a significant wellspring of protein, and assuming you select them cautiously, you will not gorge the fats in them. Moreover, meat is worthwhile because of its ability to fulfill hunger really. However, it should never be fried, and it should always be prepared in healthy ways, such as roasting, sautéing, grilling, baking, broiling, or broiling. Instead of butter or other oils when sautéing, use a small amount of healthy fats like extra virgin olive oil or canola oil.

The leanest cuts of meat include sirloin (counting ground), tenderloin, top flank, round tip, base round, eye round, and top round. These are the least fatty cuts of meat. Lean, well-trimmed pork chops or tenderloin are acceptable alternatives. Boiled ham is acceptable at this point. Because it is leaner, Canadian bacon is preferred to American bacon. Veal chops, cutlets, top round, and trimmed leg of lamb are all permissible.

Anything low in fat or without fat is ideal when shopping for meats for a lunch gathering. Boiling ham is not allowed, but honey-cured or honey-processed ham is. Believe it or not, pastrami can be acceptable if you can locate a lean variety. It is legal to eat salami and low-fat bologna. Additionally acceptable are cut turkey chest, turkey wieners, and turkey salami.

Cornish game hen, turkey breast, and chicken breast are sufficient for poultry. Dim meat is allowed in small quantities in Stage 2.

Canadian bacon and turkey bacon are acceptable for breakfast meats. Due to the submerged fat it contains, standard bacon is only allowed in extremely small quantities. Breakfast wieners are the same way; Turkey-based variations, such as links or patties, are superior to the standard variety.

Any soy-based food, including tofu, tempeh, can be utilized instead of meat at any phase of the eating regimen. Choose delicate, light, or low-fat forms. Acceptable nuts are soybeans. Burgers that are vegetarian are also allowed.

Oils: Canola oil, extra virgin olive oil, flaxseed oil, nut oil, sesame oil, and pecan oil can be used in cooking and salad dressings on each of the three stages.

Pasta: Pasta isn't permitted in Stage 1.

Rice: In Phase 1, no rice is permitted.

Snacks: Limit sweets to 75 calories per day during Stage 1. Try to find sugar-free, hard candy; baking powder made without sugar; Popsicles made without sugar; Popsicles made without adding sugar; gelatin free of sugar; also, gum without sugar.

In Phase 1, even macadamia nuts, which we used to think were bad for you, are okay. Despite their high nutrient content, almonds should only be consumed in small amounts throughout the day.

Soups: Clear stocks and reduced-fat canned bean soups are acceptable during Stage 1.

Sweeteners: It is possible to use any calorie-free sugar substitute.

Vegetables: Vegetables can be consumed in large quantities throughout the diet. All of the green ones can stay. Spinach and other verdant, dull-green vegetables are OK. Beans (dark, margarine, green, Italian, kidney, lentils, lima, pigeon, soy, split peas, and wax), artichokes, avocados, ringer peppers, broccoli, broccoli rabe, cabbage, cauliflower, celery, collard greens, cucumbers, eggplant, fennel, leeks, lettuce (all assortments), mushrooms (different types), onions, radishes, scallions, and shallot

Looking for Stage 2? Stage 2 is where you'll start eating after the first 14 days of the South Ocean Side Diet. In this subsequent stage, you can consume all of the food varieties from Stage 1 or more increases.

I always advise dieters to gradually reintroduce new carbohydrates, such as a cup of rice or pasta once or twice a week or one piece of fruit per day. If you need bread, you should eat whole grain varieties that are real.

Assuming you once again introduce more starches into your eating regimen and notice that your weight reduction eases back, you've likely gone excessively far. On the other hand, you are free to regularly indulge in a slice of bread without putting your hard work at risk.

You can purchase the going with things during Stage 2:

Products baked: This may be the most perplexing passageway in the grocery store. You'll get the impression that you're getting a healthy meal because the bread will be made with 7-, 9-, and even 12-grain grains. However, if you look at the ingredient list, you'll notice that enriched white flour is at the top, which is against the rules. Whole grain bread, which is always available in health food stores, is something you should try to find. After that, look for bread that only contains whole wheat flour. Other options include multigrain, oat-bran, rye, and whole wheat breads. There should be at least 3 grams of fiber in each slice of bread. Consider this more carefully because certain manufacturers will provide the information per serving, which is significant for two cuts.)

Whole-grain wheat flatbreads and saltines are plentiful and suitable for Stages 2 and 3. Pita bread continues to taste good after 14 days. Look for wheat varieties that have been stone-ground or whole. Little, entire grain bagels are adequate for Stage 2.

In general, I suggest consuming a few starches each day. Supper can incorporate earthy colored rice, and lunch can incorporate a cut of entire grain bread. Possibly whole-wheat pasta and squashed yams for one meal. Try to pair each of these carbs with healthy proteins like cheese, fish, or meat. Fats slow the rate at which your body processes sugars, making them useful to consume.

Breads and prepared foods should not contain hydrogenated oils.

Supper rolls, refined wheat bread, refined wheat bagels, and white bread should never be eaten.

Beverages: Phase 2: Stay away from all beverages with added sugar and fruit juices. It is acceptable to drink a few glasses of white or red wine each day. Because It slows the rate at which your blood sugar rises, it is best to drink wine with a meal. However, lager ought to in any case be kept away from. It raises glucose much more quickly than table sugar. Even light beers are prohibited. Alongside all premixed blended drinks, whiskey additionally goes to sugar and ought to be kept away from.

Cereals: Oats that are cooked in the conventional manner in the oven are acceptable, but instant or microwave versions should be avoided. Although some cold cereals, like Kellogg's All-Bran with Extra Fiber, can be considered healthy, the majority lack sufficient sugar and fiber. Despite its healthy reputation, even granola typically contains too much sugar. The term "fat-free" refers to cereals, but the problem lies in the bad carbs and sugar, not the fat.

Even in Phase 2, cornflakes should be avoided.

Dressings, toppings, and flavors: honey mustard, barbecue sauce, ketchup, and any other sugar, corn syrup, molasses, or high-fructose corn syrup-based condiment or sauce; without fat-laden mayonnaise, salad dressings, ready-made grill sauces, and other similar items; Additionally, relish and sweet pickles have not yet been accepted.

Dairy: The basic guidelines from Stage 1 remain. You can also add nonfat yogurt that has been altered to make it look better, one 4-ounce serving per day.

Fish and shellfish: Consuming a lot of fish and shellfish that have been cooked in healthy ways is still a good idea.

Flour: In Stage 2, whole wheat flour can be used again. There are many different kinds of flour that can be found in supermarkets, including whole wheat flour, buckwheat flour, rye flour, barley flour, and others. Soybean and chickpea flours are also used to make healthy flours. In addition, these grains can be substituted for enriched white flours in many boxed mixes for bread, pancakes, and other baked goods. Simply ensure that the mixes do not contain any hydrogenated oils.

Fruit: Right now, it's fine to appreciate fruit. There are strawberry, blueberry, apple, cantaloupe, cherry, grapefruit, grapes, mangoes, oranges, peaches, pears, and plums to choose from. There are kiwis, grapefruit, and grapefruit choices. During Stage 2, all sugared jams, juice- or syrup-pressed canned natural products, bananas, pineapple, raisins, and watermelon should be avoided.

Poultry and meat: In Phase 2, you can still savor the delectable meats and poultry from Phase 1. The consumption of pâté and other types of fatty birds should continue.

Oils: In Phase 2, use the oils we used in Phase 1 sparingly.

Pasta: Phase 1 approves it if it is made with whole wheat flour.

Rice: White rice is never permitted; You'll feel safer if you eat basmati rice, which has an earthy color and is actually a seed rather than rice. Second rice is not a good option.

Snacks: In Stage 2, return to your diet sparingly by selecting ambivalent and semisweet chocolate. Puddings without sugar or fat are another favorite. An unbelievable snack for Stage 2 is sans oil air-popped popcorn. Pretzels, potato chips, cookies, cupcakes, and other sweet and salty snacks should be avoided.

Soup: In Stage 2, you can eat canned bean soup because it does not contain pasta or any other starch. Powdered soups are generally not a good idea due to the high amount of carbohydrates they contain.

Sweeteners: After Stage 1, honey and molasses can be used again with some caution, but other sugars should only be used for special occasions.

Vegetables: Sweet potatoes, carrots, and yams can be included in your diet once more right now. Beets, corn, and white potatoes ought to in any case be kept away from. Again, take it easy at first and keep track of how much and how often you want these vegetables.

Breaking the Rules You might be surprised to learn that some of the recipes in this book use relatively small amounts of ingredients that are either "off limits" during a specific phase of the diet or "off limits" in general. Phase 3 cheesecake uses 12 cups of white sugar, Phase 3 quick bread uses 1 cup of white flour, Phase 1 beef and pepper salad uses 1 tablespoon of dry sherry, and so on. Because they fundamentally enhance the flavor or surface of a dish, we do include these food sources when they are actually used. Additionally, because the initial small amount is distributed across multiple servings, you do not consume the entire amount in your portion.

However, just as important, these two recipes demonstrate that the South Pacific Diet can be incorporated into a lifestyle with just the right amount of adaptability. If you follow the healthy rules of your stage, your weight loss and overall health goals shouldn't be affected in the long run.

Made in the USA
Las Vegas, NV
22 December 2024

15221621R00075